CITADEL

THE TRUE STORY OF ONE MAN'S
WAR AGAINST THE PIRATES OF SOMALIA

JORDAN WYLIE

Mirror Books

Published by Mirror Books,
an imprint of Trinity Mirror plc,
1 Canada Square,
London E14 5AP, England

www.mirrorbooks.com
twitter.com/themirrorbooks

Mirror Books 2017

© Jordan Wylie

The rights of Jordan Wylie to be identified as the author
of this book has been asserted, in accordance with the Copyright,
Designs and Patents Act 1988.

ISBN 9781907324741

First paperback edition

Printed and bound in Great Britain
by CPI Group (UK) Ltd, Croydon, CR0 4YY

Every effort has been made to fulfil requirements with regard to
reproducing copyright material. The author and publisher will be
glad to rectify any omissions at the earliest opportunity.

CONTENTS

Jordan Wylie is a former British soldier who served in the UK Armed Forces for almost 10 years as an intelligence and armoured reconnaissance specialist. His military service included operations in Iraq and Northern Ireland.

Since leaving the military in 2009, Jordan has built a successful career as a maritime security and risk management consultant, providing expert advice to the international shipping industry, governments and private security companies worldwide on training, capacity building programmes and risk mitigation.

In 2017, Jordan was highly commended as an unsung hero of the shipping industry at the international safety at sea awards, for his exceptional work on raising awareness of emerging cyber security threats to the marine and offshore sectors.

Jordan holds a BA (Hons) in Security & Risk Management, an MA in Maritime Security and is the current president of the Security & Risk Management Alumni. In addition, Jordan is an ambassador for the Chennai 6 campaign for justice and a trustee and volunteer at 'Horse Power', the regimental museum of The King's Royal Hussars.

Further information about Jordan including contact details can be found at: www.jordanwylie.org

To my daughter Evie Grace, my greatest
achievement in life, and to my parents for their
inspiration, guidance, support and
all the love a son could wish for.

MORE PRAISE FOR 'CITADEL'

'CITADEL tells a tale. How Private Military Contractors stopped the Somali pirates dead in their tracks, going against the then prevailing wisdoms, and against powerful vested interests. Jordan Wylie was a key player in this. His amazing story is well told here'
SIMON MANN, Former SAS Officer, Mercenary and Author

'Private security forces worked halfway between international navies and merchant shipping crews on the pirate-infested Indian Ocean. Some governments thought they were cowboys; some pirates thought they were imperialist mercenaries. But most of these men were professional and experienced veterans that were instrumental in bringing an end to the surge of piracy off Somalia in the early twenty-first century, and Jordan Wylie's fascinating book tells us how'
MICHAEL SCOTT MOORE, Former Somali Pirate Hostage,
Journalist and Author of 'Sweetness and Blood'

'Jordan Wylie continues to develop his niche in this world and Citadel is a must-read for those seeking inspiration and adventure. Citadel is a wealth of first-hand knowledge on the methodologies of Somali piracy and although attacks have subsided off the Horn of Africa, piracy will never be fully eradicated neither globally nor in the Indian Ocean. Citadel therefore should be regarded as a manual for lessons learned that will remain relevant to the maritime community in the present day as well as for the foreseeable future. Given his determination and ambition as well as taking into account his journey from where he started to where he is now, I am confident we will hear of many more positive experiences from Jordan Wylie'
KARSTEN VON HOESSLIN, Host of National Geographic's Lawless Oceans Series

'An action packed and inspiring true story, highlighting danger, passion and drive throughout'
ASH DYKES, Adventurer and Extreme Athlete

'Unbeknownst to the majority, our global economy pivots on the freedom of international shipping and the ability to move goods anywhere in the world at any time. Citadel exposes the value of that trade, the risks resulting from those that covet that value and the resource needed to protect it. A cracking read in every respect.'
REAR ADMIRAL NICK LAMBERT RN (Retired), Blue Economy Advocate

'From playing football with Jordan nearly 20 years ago to seeing what he does today is incredible. I have found Citadel a fascinating insight into an unknown world, a very intense and action-packed thriller based on real events'
RICKIE LAMBERT, England International Footballer

'Jordan was one of my most experienced team leaders during the height of piracy, always professional and respected by the captains and crews he worked with. They would often specifically request him for their vessels. Jordan successfully repelled several hostile pirate attacks for my clients and kept their people and cargo safe. His personal story is an excellent account of the highs and lows of private maritime security operations, warts and all'
WILL McMANUS Former British Army Officer and Legionnaire, Maritime Security Company CEO

Acknowledgements

My grateful thanks are due to the following people.

Above all to Alan Clark, who has skilfully extracted my memories, thoughts and feelings and shaped them into a coherent story. This book would not have been possible without him.

To General Sir Richard Shirreff KCB CBE for so kindly providing an extremely generous foreword to the book.

To all the friends and colleagues, both maritime security professionals and military personnel, alongside whom I had the immense honour of serving and who have allowed me to use their real names and helped make sure this book is an accurate account.

To everyone at my publisher Mirror Books who has made this such an enjoyable experience: publishing director Paula Scott; executive editor Jo Sollis; book editor Charlotte Cole; art director Julie Adams and the marketing team of Cynthia Hamilton and Melanie Sambells.

To William MacLachlan and Richard Neylon from HFW for providing legal advice and guidance on maritime security issues and for telling me 'how it is' when I needed it most.

To the late Giles Noakes of BIMCO for the inspirational work he did in the fight against Somali piracy; rest in peace.

CITADEL

To all the amazing, dedicated seafarers who ensure that international trade and commerce keep moving every day. They really do make the world go round.

And finally, to the people of Somalia, even those involved in piracy, most of whom only ever want a better life and some hope for a brighter future. I hope they will soon find it.

Some names of vessels have been changed

Foreword

By General Sir Richard Shirreff KCB CBE,
Former Deputy Supreme Allied Commander Europe

This is the story of an exceptional individual. Born and brought up on a Blackpool council estate, Jordan Wylie owes his remarkable success to three factors: the strength of his family, in particular the example of his Royal Marine, Falklands veteran father; his time as a cavalryman in The King's Royal Hussars; his own innate ability coupled with energy, drive and persistence. This book is an inspiring example of sustained achievement against the odds. But it is more than that: as a former Non-Commissioned Officer in The King's Royal Hussars, Jordan Wylie exemplifies the spirit of the cavalry; tough, versatile, quick-thinking and adaptable.

Unable to achieve his lifelong ambitions as a soldier due to injury, Jordan Wylie made his mark in the world of maritime security in that most ruthless of struggles, the protection of shipping against the scourge of Somali piracy. 'Citadel' tells the story of the reality of his experiences at the sharp end, in the forefront of that fight, initially as a security guard on ships attacked by pirates. But it goes further than that. His story and subsequent success highlight the strategic importance of the private sector in maritime security operations, complementing the efforts of the armada of ships from NATO, the EU and others in countering what came close to causing the collapse of the shipping industry off the Horn of Africa and in the Indian Ocean. In a world facing increasingly complex and challenging security threats on the one hand and Western governments reluctant to spend any more than the minimum on their security forces on the other, Jordan Wylie's experience highlights the value of properly trained, legal and ethically based private security companies capable of being deployed to protect our people and assets. More broadly, the strategic issue is that the West cannot ignore failed and failing states such as Somalia.

What was a 'gold rush' for many ex-soldiers seeking their fortunes in the growth of private sector security soon ended as international maritime operations, combined with best practice in the shipping industry first contained, and then neutralized, the threat of Somali piracy. For many, this was the end of the game. But for Jordan Wylie, his experience was the foundation of what has become an inspirational career. As well as an exciting read, 'Citadel' is a lesson in how to approach the challenge of life by a man who, I am in no doubt, will continue to build on his success.

Prologue

'Oi, my lad!' he yelled. 'Put that away or you'll be nicked.'

There are many challenges in this life. Many are achievable, some downright impossible. Firmly in the latter category I would place any attempt to stop a pee in mid-flow after several bottles of cider, even when requested to do so by a member of Her Majesty's Constabulary for the County of Lancashire.

'If you don't sod off, I'll piss on you,' I replied, with the cheery arrogance of a sozzled 14-year-old.

The copper waited patiently till I'd shaken the drops off then demanded my name and date of birth.

'My name is John Smith,' I replied, with an embarrassing lack of imagination, 'and my dad's a former Royal Marine. If you touch me, he'll come and knock you out.' That did it. I was on my way to the cells. Shit. But how weird it seems, looking back now, that something so ordinary, and of course a bit tacky, could trigger one of those moments when we freeze in our tracks, look at ourselves and decide to take a different road.

It'd been a Friday afternoon much like any other. I'd told Mum I'd been invited for a meal and a sleepover at a mate's. Nothing unusual about that. It's so easy to lie when you're trusted.

The usual bunch of us had headed for the park. After school, it was our venue of choice. The park was vast, hundreds of acres of open space, a great green lung in the midst of the cramped, grey streets in which we all lived. There were sports fields, a big boating lake and fancy Italian gardens with fountains and statues.

We did the usual, slightly aimless stuff that you do when you're just 'hanging out'; having a fag, terrorising old dears out walking their dogs, all the usual 'little shit' behaviour. We'd often play 'spin the bottle', where the boy and girl beside whom the bottle stopped were required to have a public snog. The booze would always be at the heart of it. As well as the cider, we'd be on the vodka and the Bacardi too, sometimes mixed together; not a great idea. If you were trying to impress some girl, it was a right passion-killer to suddenly honk all over her shoes. Trouble was that you probably needed the booze to give you the courage to chat her up in the first place, so it was a bit of a vicious circle.

But finding yourself frogmarched into a police station sobers you up pretty fast. Reality hits you like a bucket of ice-cold water. Your mates are no longer there to cheer you on. Suddenly you're on your own, feeling very small and very scared. It's surprising how frightening a police cell can be. It's only a small room after all, but not the sort of room you're used to. There's no comfort to be found in it. No pictures on the wall, no curtains at the tiny window. Just a hard wooden chair, a thin mattress and a blanket that would presumably be your bed. A bucket in the corner. Bloody hell. It's a room stripped down to the bare bones. A bit like how you feel in yourself; all the bravado having drained out of you like the cider you'd pissed into the gutter.

If you're honest, you want your mum, though you're shit scared of what she's going to say when she gets hold of you. Not to mention your dad. Oh God. Dad.

So you sit there in silence, wondering what happens now. The only sounds you hear scare you even more; the heavy footsteps that march past the locked door of your cell, the occasional shouts of some nutter who's banged up nearby.

Eventually the heavy door swings open and the duty-sergeant comes in. He looks down at you as if you were something he's found on the sole of his shoe. He's having a long day and he's been dealing with little gits like you since long before you were born.

'Well, we've spoken to your dad,' he says, 'and he's told us to keep you here as long as we want.'

I pictured Dad's face as he'd said this to the police. He'd not have exploded; it wasn't his way. He'd just have said it with quiet determination and put the phone down.

In the end, I was banged up for 16 long, unforgettable hours. It gave me plenty of time to think about the parties I'd been to, where the police had arrived and arrested one of the older lads for drugs, burglary or breaching bail conditions. As I'd watched them being carted off, I'd even thought how cool they were. But now the local nick didn't seem remotely cool any longer. Eventually I was hauled out to the desk and given a formal caution for being drunk and disorderly. The joy of walking out of that police station into the fresh air was like being reborn. It was a place I never wanted to see again. But there was no escape from the massive bollocking that now came from my father. 'Are you trying to ruin your life?' he asked. 'Do you want to end up in Strangeways?' 'It was just a bit of fun Dad.' 'Oh really?

Was it fun being locked in a police cell then?' 'Nope'.

'And you lied to your mother about where you were and what you were doing.' 'Yeah, I'm sorry.'

'Well now you've got a record down the nick. The police know who you are. Are you proud of that? We didn't raise you as well as we could to see you go the way of so many others round here. Is that what you want?' 'No Dad.' If I'd felt small in the police cell, I felt so much smaller now. What my father couldn't understand was why anyone wouldn't try to make the very best of themselves. He just couldn't get that. He'd achieved a lot in his life and he had four military service medals to prove it. But everything he'd achieved, he'd accomplished by himself, often against huge odds. My dad was, in every way, my hero. And now I'd let him down. I'd diminished myself in his eyes and that hurt like a punch in the guts.

As I stood there in front of my parents, tired, hungover and utterly miserable, I promised myself that I'd do my damndest to never disappoint them again. From now on, my life would be about making them proud of me. At the age of 14, I had no idea how I was going to achieve that. I just hoped that, sometime in the future, an opportunity would appear out of nowhere and give me the chance. But it was going to be a good few years, and a long bumpy road, before I found it.

CHAPTER 1

Blackpool Boy

'What the hell are you doing here, Jordan?'

It wasn't the first occasion in my life I'd asked myself that question. I'd asked it on my first day at army training camp, getting out of bed at 5am to be shouted at by some grumpy bastard of a sergeant. I'd asked it when I'd arrived in Northern Ireland and clocked the signs everywhere warning me to 'beware of snipers and mortar attacks'. And I'd sure as hell asked it in Iraq when the bullets were actually whizzing past my innocent young head. Shit, these people were actually trying to kill me. But this time, the question seemed bigger than ever. This time, there were no screaming sergeants, marching feet or whizzing bullets. Now I was asking myself that question into a great dark void, into an almost overwhelming silence.

Standing night-watch on the bridge-wing of a huge ship as it edged across a deserted sea was a lonely experience. Okay, you weren't totally alone; there were one or two guys a few metres away in the wheelhouse, steering the ship. But it was different for them. They'd got their comfy seats, their cheery panels of flashing lights, their radars and each other's chatter. You were outside on the open-air platform that stretched out on either side of the wheelhouse, like the wings of a seagull. There was danger out there in the darkness. That's why the decks were bordered with razor-wire and hoses were primed and ready to pump high-pressure jets of water into the faces of the enemy. You needed to stay wide awake; there was no greater disgrace than falling asleep on the job. All you had were your own thoughts and, if you were lucky, the occasional cup of coffee.

If there was a moon, it wasn't so bad. At least the moon lit up the waves, let you glimpse the far horizon, gave you some sense of perspective. But when there was no moon, the stars were clouded over and there was no discernible line between the sea and sky, it could feel like you were being suffocated by a blanket of blackness. All you could see, all that helped you feel grounded, was the deck of the ship way down below. Unlike most passenger ships, the bridge on modern tankers and container vessels was located in the superstructure right at the stern. The cargo deck stuck out in front like some gigantic tongue of iron and steel, pushing its way into the mouth of the waves. There were some navigation lights, of course, but they were feeble, cold and functional; not exactly Blackpool Illuminations.

So it was basically just you and whatever came into your head. And it was easy for the blackness in front of you to turn itself into a kind of blank screen; the people and places you cared about appearing on it like in a movie. I saw my partner Laura and our baby daughter Evie. Mum and Dad. Nana and Grandad. Mates from home, mates from the army. I imagined what they might be doing. I pictured the rooms they might be in. I saw Evie playing in the garden; Mum, the football fanatic, glued to *Match Of The Day* while Dad did his crossword; the lads out on Blackpool prom, buying kebabs to soak up the beers. How far away they seemed that night as I stood on the bridge-wing in the middle of the Indian Ocean. After my long years in the army, we were well used to being separated by now. But it had never been easy; it had always taken its toll. And now here I was again, thousands of miles from everything that mattered.

'So what are you doing here, Jordan?'

I was born and raised in a town with two faces. A schizophrenic place. For people who've never been there, the name Blackpool conjures up the Tower and the promenade, the famous Illuminations, the fairgrounds, the variety theatres, the donkey rides and all that stuff. The 'Las Vegas of the North', they'd once called it. A place for fun and getting away from it all.

But there's another Blackpool just behind the glitter. Like most British holiday resorts, the sudden availability of cheap package holidays abroad in the 60s and 70s had dealt it a devastating blow. Blackpool didn't quite die but, from then on, it was certainly on permanent life support. A mile inland from the gaudy lights of the seashore was a town overshadowed by deprivation, high rates of drug abuse, crime and teenage pregnancy (even today, 30 years on, Blackpool GPs dole out more anti-depressants than anywhere else in the country.) It was a place where it was all too easy for a lad to find himself going off the straight and narrow and where nobody would be very surprised if he did.

The family I came from wasn't exactly poor, but we'd never had it cushy either. My first few years were spent in Grange Park, one of the biggest council estates in the north of England. When I was born in 1983, it was a shabby neighbourhood with a lousy reputation and facing a fistful of challenges; high unemployment, low educational stand-ards, a run-down environment. But I guess when you're young, you can cope with most things. I didn't really grasp how rough it was, it was just what was 'normal'. I had two sisters, one older, one younger and a large extended family who all lived nearby; an assorted tribe of grandparents, aunties, uncles and cousins. Whatever I might have lacked materially, I could never say I wasn't loved.

Not much was expected of Grange Park kids. Few would be applying to study at Oxford or Cambridge. Most of us would end up as factory-fodder or in other low-paid jobs. Maybe we'd marry too young and have children we couldn't afford, drifting into debt and looking for dodgy ways of putting things right.

In the years after my own teenage brush with the law, I saw guys I knew beginning to head in the wrong direction, on that grim path that would eventually lead some of them straight to the magistrates' court and maybe the great grim gates of Strangeways Prison. These were the boys I'd drunk cider with in Stanley Park, played football with, ridden on the dodgems with. If I'd needed any examples of Dad's dire warnings, there were plenty around me. Among them were a few members of my own extended family.

The matriarch of our family was my mother's mother. Nana was a wonderful woman. Nobody could make my favourite baked potato with cheese and onion like she could. She always said exactly what she thought, often loudly and in public, much to the embarrassment of Grandad, but she was always loving and supportive to each

4

and every one of us, which somehow made it even worse that some of her grandchildren were not exactly 'kind' to her. One of them was always in and out of the nick, his own poor mother spending more than she could afford travelling to visit him. Christ knows why she bothered. I couldn't believe I'd ever remotely admired these 'cool' guys. I watched it all and kept my distance.

After my big scare though, I hadn't instantly become a perfect little angel. That would have been pretty much impossible in Blackpool anyway; the lure of the prom was just too strong. I still hung out with my mates in the amusement arcades 'feeding the lights' of the fruit machines. I worked on the pleasure beach, at the booths with names like 'The Arabian Derby', where holidaymakers would waste their money trying to win a giant Bugs Bunny or Mickey Mouse. I was taught all the tricks and scams to make sure they rarely got a prize; if they did, the boss would take it out of your wages. For a while, some friends and I even pitched a wheelbarrow at the North Pier and sold yo-yos that lit up.

'Up, down, all around. Light-up yo-yos only a pound!' I had to shout out. ' Buy from me – batteries free! Don't be gloomy, get yourself a loomy!'

Some nights I could make £50. It was amazing the total rubbish that people would buy when they were out on a stag night or a hen night, well-oiled from the pubs.

So nobody I knew would have guessed that Jordan Wylie had suddenly become saintly. But Dad's dire warnings were now never far from the front of my mind. Not to mention the disappointment I'd seen in his eyes that day.

I reckon it had finally come home to me just how lucky I

was. Both my parents were, and still are, exceptional people. I'd been blessed with the best role models any kid could wish for. Neither of them had had it easy, but they'd risen above anything life had thrown at them. Mum had spent most of her life in menial jobs; working as a hospital cleaner and serving in a fish and chip shop. Her escape from all that was, amazingly, football. Not just watching it, playing it. She captained Blackpool Ladies Team for many years and played for England seven times. An incredible left winger, she was still kicking a ball well into her fifties, trying to conceal any injuries she suffered from Dad, in case he told her it was time to hang up her boots before she broke her neck. Dad had come from an estate in Preston that was even more notorious than Grange Park. He'd been one of 10 children, so parental affection had been spread pretty thin. He'd served in the Royal Marines for 15 years and seen action in the Falklands, something about which he rarely spoke, and had then taken a degree to become a technical illustrator in the construction business.

They were the most unselfish of parents, always putting their kids before themselves. Happy to sacrifice their own well-earned holiday so my sisters and I could go on school trips. They once drove me all the way to Belgium for a school football match, then turned right round again without even seeing the game, because they had to get back for work. We might not have been rich, but Mandy and David Wylie gave me a moral compass, even if I had mislaid it for a little while. I know now that they couldn't have given me anything of greater value. My big stroke of luck was that two such special people bumped into each other and then got married.

Like Mum, my major talent as a kid had been football. I'd been bloody good in fact. I was obsessed with it; could think of nothing else. I started at the age of six and won the Golden Boot Award as top scorer in every amateur team I ever played for (and still do today). I joined the youth team of Blackpool FC then, at the age of 13, was signed up by their arch-rivals Preston North End, who weren't impressed when I turned up for training in a Blackpool kit. Dad used to give me a pocket-money supplement of 50 pence for every goal I scored and a fiver for a hat-trick. Later I was signed up by another Blackpool team called Spirit of Youth, where I scored 52 goals in one season. I took part in foreign tours to the USA and Asia; I even played on the sacred turf of the old Wembley. All this attracted the attention of scouts from some big clubs. I was offered trials for both Manchester City and Wimbledon. Mum and Dad were thrilled and so was I; here was something I could do to make them proud of me. The trials seemed to be okay, but then the typewritten letters plopped through the letterbox. I raced to pick them up off the doormat, Dad and Mum right behind me.

'Well?' they asked in unison. But my face gave them the answer.

'Never mind love,' said Mum, sliding an arm round me.

'It's only a game, Jord,' said Dad, knowing full well that was a bare-faced fib. In our house, the great Bill Shankly's famous comment certainly applied.

'Some people think football is a matter of life and death. I assure you, it's much more serious than that.'

So I had to take it on the chin that my dreams of being a star of 'the beautiful game' were never going to happen. And it was nobody's fault but my own. When I should have eaten a healthy chicken salad and been in bed by 7pm the night before a match, I'd been out with my pals on the prom, chatting up the girls and eating cod and chips. It was that typical teenage waywardness raising its head again. The 'lad' thing. Once more, I needed to learn that there was a price to pay for everything. My footballing talent hadn't failed me, but my character had, just as it had done when I'd landed in the police cell. I have old mates playing in today's Premier League who still swear I was a better footballer than they were, but that I didn't have the discipline. It taught me that the things you really wanted in this world wouldn't just fall into your lap, you had to graft for them or they would simply move out of your reach. Years later, when Blackpool got into the Premier League, I visited a tattooist.

'So what's it to be?' he asked as I rolled up my left trouser leg.

'This', I replied, handing him a printout of the club crest.

So now I have the motto *'Progress'* emblazoned on my hairy shin, reminding me every day that everything that happens to you has a purpose, especially the stuff you get wrong. You fuck-up. You learn the lesson. You move forwards. That's progress.

But even though a football career was lost forever, I'd managed to scrape enough GCSEs to study sports science at college. The course was focused on understanding how the footballer's body works, taking temperatures, analysing tactics and all that jazz. But football to me meant being out on the pitch with the wind in your face and the goal in your sights. Nothing else. I got my diploma, but I just wasn't cut out to be any sort of backroom boy. I'd once pictured myself marrying a Spice Girl, so sticking a thermometer up some bloke's hairy arse wasn't much of a compensation.

One day, with another guy from college who was as disenchanted as I was, I wandered into the Army Careers Office. A bloke I knew from school was behind the desk and he gave us the hard sell. My college mate decided it wasn't for him, but I was hooked and went on for a formal interview. I liked the idea of the Military Police, but I failed the psychometric tests. Not the right sort of brain, they said. My only possibilities were the infantry or the cavalry; in other words, as a front-line trooper. Mum of course was panicking, convinced I'd be killed within a week. Despite his own military career, Dad didn't push me, quietly suggesting I look at the RAF and the Royal Marines as well. But I didn't really need any pushing. Following in the footsteps of a man like my father would surely be the best possible thing I could do.

So, like many thousands of 18 year-olds, I turned to the forces as a way of finding a direction. I'd known a good few from the backstreets of Blackpool who'd done just that. It wasn't about 'escaping' from who you were or where you came from. I was proud of my roots and always would be. It was just about seeing what else might be out there and where a new path might lead you.

But Christ, it was tough at first. Really tough. A long way from Mum's cooking and a nice lie-in whenever I felt like it. It was an alien environment and, for the first few weeks at training camp in Winchester, I bloody hated it. After a month, I was ready to quit. Then I got a short leave home.

'Nothing worth having ever came easy,' Dad said. 'Basic training isn't typical of army life. Stick with it till the end of the course and if you still can't take it, come out. But what will you do then? Ask yourself that.'

The answer was only too clear when I went back into my local pubs and saw the same guys propping up the same bar, telling the same jokes. I knew that most of them would still be in that pub in 30 years' time, older and greyer, with sod all to show for their lives. Shit, I wanted more for myself than that. I went back to camp with a whole new attitude. I somehow flicked a switch in my brain and buckled down to it like you wouldn't believe. I even won the 'most improved recruit' award; a back-handed compliment if ever there was one. By the end of those three months, I realised that my desire for success was stronger than my fear of failure. My passing-out parade in Winchester, with Mum and Dad watching me, was a brilliant moment. I hoped my Dad was thinking that, whatever happened to me now, at least I'd avoided that cell in Strangeways.

I really believed this was it. My future sorted. One day, I'd be a regimental sergeant-major. One day, I'd march again on this very parade-ground, shouting out the drill to a bunch of newbies, just like I was now. By that time, I'd have a good few rings on my bark, stripes on my shoulders and medals on my chest. I'd have seen action in some war or other and been mentioned in dispatches. I'd be a man respected by everyone. A pillar of the regiment. Hey, Jordan Wylie's future was all mapped out now. It never crossed my mind that sometimes even detailed maps lead you to a dead end.

CHAPTER 2

Birth of a Soldier

After my bumpy beginning, missing Mum's mollycoddling and generally being a bit of a twat, I soon discovered that the army was, next to my Dad, the best teacher I ever had. It taught me respect for others and respect for myself. The core values drummed into you in the services stand you in good stead not just on parade-grounds and battlefields, but in almost every aspect of your life. You learn integrity, loyalty, discipline, selfless commitment, courage and respect. That list may sound dead stuffy, pompous even, but these are gifts you can't put a price on. Once they're in your DNA, you've got them forever.

In my case, the man who did most to put them there was a corporal called Jon Neve. He was only a few years older than me but he was what they called a 'flyer', a soldier of outstanding qualities chosen to mentor raw recruits and be a role model for everything they should aim to be. In his attitudes to hard work and discipline, in his determination to do his best, both for himself and for others, he was the polar opposite of some of the aimless bad-lads I'd known back home. However unpromising the material, Jon was undaunted and somehow he turned this grumpy, homesick boy into a tolerable new soldier.

When basic training was over, I became a trooper in the

King's Royal Hussars. In its upper echelons, it was a dead posh regiment. Rich, well-connected blokes with hyphenated surnames and monikers like Tristram and Rupert; we even had a cousin of The Queen. But I soon noticed that class differences mattered much less than I expected. There was a mutual appreciation of the roles each man played in the team. I started to rub up against people I'd never have met in a million years in civilian life. For the first time, my horizons began to stretch way beyond Lancashire.

The King's Royal Hussars was a cavalry regiment, but the horses had long since been put out to pasture and these days we rode tanks. My first task was learning how to drive one of these 62-ton monsters. It might sound exciting but it was a tough job. An armoured battle-tank had very little in common with a Ford Mondeo. You lay flat on your back, looking up through a periscope. As the driver, you were responsible for the comfort and safety of the tank commander, the operator and the gunner up above. If your driving was too bumpy, you might well get a kick in the head. 'For fuck's sake Wylie, are you trying to bring up my breakfast?'

Not long after my training, I got sent to Northern Ireland for six months' operational tour. By then, in 2002, the worst of the Troubles was over, but the legacy of those terrible times still hung in the air like a bad smell. As we got off the helicopter, there were signs everywhere warning us to be on our guard at all times. Christ, this was serious stuff. The peace process was still fragile, I was here to play my tiny part in keeping it and I felt that responsibility. As we arrived, the Parachute Regiment was just leaving.

'We wish you a Merry Christmas', they sang at us new

arrivals as they headed for home, like a gang of big kids released from school. I survived Northern Ireland without a scratch, either physically or emotionally, but Iraq was to be a different matter. The 'war' itself had lasted only a few months, but the British Army presence, so controversial back home, went on for years.

I was 22 by now, had been promoted to lance-corporal and had spent six months in intensive training before being deployed there. I was going to need it.

Our camp was at Al Amarah, a sizeable city on the River Tigris, on the road between Baghdad and Basra, close to the border with Iran. At first, its citizens had welcomed their liberation from the tyranny of Saddam Hussein, but it was a place of complex religious and tribal loyalties and, as time passed, they'd turned against the British forces, seeing them instead as occupiers rather than liberators.

Now Al Amarah was possibly the most dangerous billet in Iraq, witnessing some of the army's fiercest fighting against the insurgents. It was here that Private Johnson Beharry had won his Victoria Cross and where six military policemen had been cornered and slaughtered by a rampaging mob. For the seven long months I was posted here, they fired 107mm Chinese rockets at us day and night.

The camp, in a dusty wasteland to the south of the city, was home to about 600 military and support staff. It wasn't an appealing place. Most of the buildings were the Portakabin type which, if you were lucky, had aircon for a few hours a day; the rest of the time you just fried like an egg. At night, I slept in a tent under a mosquito net. It was pretty basic.

Right after my arrival in April 2005, on my very first

patrol, I was caught up in what could have become a serious incident. As lance-corporal, I was in charge of a team of seven or eight junior soldiers, none older than about 19 and one of them a female medic. The British Army's maps of these border areas didn't exactly tally with those of the Iranians and one day we found ourselves in what they clearly considered was Iranian territory.

Suddenly, bullets were flying past us. No matter how many times you've fired your weapon in training, nothing quite prepares you for the first time somebody shoots back. It's almost unreal. Every expletive you'd not want your mother to hear flies out of your mouth. As a leader, I had all these young faces looking anxiously to me for orders. Christ. We started firing back, then quickly ran for cover behind a ridge, before mounting our vehicle and getting the hell out of there. Every 10 seconds seemed to last an hour. Eventually the Iranians had the wit to realise that we meant no harm and stopped shooting. Back at the camp, quite a few people were cheerfully pissed off that I'd seen some action on my very first patrol. So much of army life is tedious and repetitive, endlessly preparing for things that may never happen, that soldiers crave action like a man craves water in the desert. You hardly allow yourself to think about the possible consequences. You're a soldier after all. Just there to do a job.

So when those unthinkable consequences do happen, it hits you hard and takes your breath away. I had a good mate called Alan Brackenbury. I'd known him for about four years. We'd served the same amount of time and had both been promoted to lance-corporal on the same day. He was a Northerner too, a Yorkshire lad, which gave us common ground. He was a relaxed guy, good at the banter, with time for everyone. In Al Amarah, we often worked out in the gym together or took a morning run round the camp. He was a fine soldier who lived for the army, had never wanted to do anything else. The sort who'd go a long way in the military life. On May 29th 2005, he went out in a three-vehicle convoy to a routine meeting with the Iraqi border police and never came back. Alan was in the leading vehicle and a roadside bomb had blown it to bits.

Four others were injured but survived. I was back at base in the Immediate Response Unit. I'd been the one who'd briefed Alan's group before it left the camp, advising on the routes they could follow. We constantly changed the routes taken by patrols in order not to set any patterns for those observing our movements. But there were only so many possible routes and the insurgents just had to get lucky once. And this time they did just that. It was me who took the initial satellite phone call from the surviving patrol commander. Jesus, it was awful. Later, when the worst of the horror had been dealt with by the exceptional medics, I went to the scene. This was the blood-soaked reality behind the spit and polish, the parade-ground preening, the black humour and the comforting conviction that, whatever happened, you'd somehow be alright.

After any major incident, a follow-up operation was quickly launched to try and catch the bastards who'd done it. There was no time to lose. Only 12 hours later, I had to debrief a roomful of 40 people, including a very senior general, some of whom had arrived pronto from Basra to help us in the search and arrest operations. The debriefing room wasn't large and it was crammed; most sitting on old wooden benches, some on the floor; all of us in helmets and body armour to protect us against the daily mortar attacks. Well-worn maps of our operational areas covered the walls. Our leaders needed to know, and fast, every tiny detail of what procedures had been followed, what intelligence might have been flawed, what needed to be learnt in order to protect the patrols being sent out today and tomorrow.

When I stood up to speak, I was only just holding myself together. The questions came thick and fast. It didn't help when the mortar siren went off in the middle of it and everybody had to hit the deck. At one point I was forced to ask for a five-minute break. I was hot, distressed, under pressure. I really didn't fancy passing out in front of everyone. The colonel followed me outside. I explained that Alan had been a good mate. He'd lost friends too, he said; in Kosovo during the Balkan Wars. It was always bloody awful but part of the soldier's lot. He was kind and supportive, even bringing me a cup of tea, before guiding me back inside. It seemed that I was still not much more than a boy after all. But by now I was growing up fast.

The atmosphere in the camp was grim. Nobody wanted to go out on patrol, but they had no choice. What made it worse was that we all knew it possibly needn't have been as bad as it was. The stripped-down Land Rover in which Alan died wasn't well armoured. Politicians in London, alarmed by the horrendous expense of a long drawn-out military presence, were always trying to cut costs; though sometimes the reason given was that heavily armoured vehicles were counterproductive in 'winning the hearts and minds' of the local population. Whatever the truth of it, Alan Brackenbury paid the price. He was only 21.

Within 48 hours of Alan's death, we were reluctantly out on patrol again, travelling on the very same routes. It was just as well we had a remarkable squadron leader in Major Nick Hunter; the sort of guy who, if he'd asked you, you'd have followed into the valley of death. The epitome of a cavalry officer, he was a gentleman of the highest calibre. Standing beside Alan's coffin, before it was flown home, he'd reminded our tense and grieving regiment of what our priorities had to be.

'The dead are gone and we will always remember them, but now let's get on and look after the living.' On this patrol I was the 'top cover' in the Land Rover, a somewhat exposed position. Under the professional exterior we were all pretty fearful; then the thing we feared most happened. With a flash and an almighty bang, another improvised explosive device (IED) exploded. For a couple of seconds, you're almost not sure if you're alive and well, alive and injured or more or less dead and on your way to paradise. When you realise you're okay, a warm wave of relief sweeps over you. When the smoke and dust clears, the sky has never looked a brighter blue, the world never more beautiful, even in a place like this.

What had saved us was that the IED had detonated 20 metres behind us; blocked by electronic countermeasures fitted to our vehicle which delayed the explosion until we were safely past it. These IEDs could be triggered in different ways; some by the vehicle breaking a beam of invisible light; others by the use of a mobile phone. It was pot luck which of these you drove into. That luck had held this time but, even when you survive it, an explosion just 20 metres away gives you a hell of a jolt, both physically and mentally.

It was a close call to say the least. How easily all our coffins might have been loaded into that plane alongside Alan Brackenbury's.

Just six weeks later, I had another brush with death. I was briefly attached as an intelligence collator to the Staffordshire regiment, a great bunch who always made you feel welcome and thought it was hilarious that a lad from Blackpool could be in the cavalry. Out on patrol, our convoy was hit. In a very similar scenario to the one in which Alan had died, there were three unarmoured Land Rovers. It was the early morning, still dark, and the flames lit up the streets. It was carnage all over again. In the event of an attack like this, my role was to provide 'all round defence' in case there was a secondary device.

Somehow, you had to switch your mind off to the fact that three of your fellow soldiers had just been blown to smithereens and focus on your job till the quick reaction force arrived on the scene. I hadn't really known the two young privates, Phil Hewett and Leon Spicer, but I'd seen their lieutenant, Richard Shearer, every day. Ex-French Foreign Legion, a professional soldier to his fingertips, a respected leader of his men, a great guy with a wonderful sense of humour. Like Alan Brackenbury, he'd lived and breathed the army since he'd been in short trousers. I still visit his memorial when I can. It was a long, terrible, day when I just had to go through the motions.

Only later, lying exhausted in my bunk, did I allow myself to think that it could have been me, that back home in Blackpool tonight there might have been a knock on the door. Mum or Dad would have answered it and known in a split second of intuition what had happened. I tried to block that image from my mind. By this point I'd been in the army for five years but it was only now that I'd come face to face with the worst of it, and these deaths, coming so close together, shook me up.

The army trains you in hundreds of different ways for every possible eventuality. But it can't really train you for dealing with death, especially death in sudden and horrific circumstances. So far, I'd been lucky, both physically and mentally. And I was never to suffer from post-traumatic stress disorder, which affected so many soldiers who'd found themselves in the vortex of awful situations. PTSD is an odd condition; sometimes people who've seen unimaginable horrors escape it entirely, while those who've not been exposed to quite such extremes, are badly hit.

'What's *he* got PTSD for?' you'd hear somebody ask. 'He's seen fuck-all action!' But it's nothing to do with how brave you might be, just the way you're wired. When life throws its worst at us, each individual spirit copes differently. I was, and still am, immensely proud to be a soldier. The first time Dad and I, both wearing our service medals, walked in the Remembrance Day parade through Blackpool was one of the best moments of my life. He'd never been a bar-room braggart, the sort who drones on about his exploits in the military; over the years he'd even managed to mislay his medals. Without telling him, I'd applied to the Ministry of Defence to issue replicas and gave them to him as a Christmas present. It was about the only time I saw Dad lose his stiff upper lip and break down. If he wasn't especially proud of himself, his family certainly were.

My years in the forces meant I'd worked with, and lived

alongside, a unique bunch of people. They weren't flawless; they had the human weaknesses we all have. Like many blokes, given half a chance, they'd drink way too much, smoke, gamble and chase women. Some of them you liked more than others. But when the time called for it, all those flaws would be quickly squashed beneath a rigid discipline and a sense of commitment to their country, their regiment, their mates and also to themselves. They did what was asked of them, even when it was beyond the call of duty, and there were times when some of them gave the most precious thing they had. In the words always used on Armistice Day, we will remember them.

It was a nasty back injury gained while serving that triggered the end of my army career. Though I struggled hard to get fully fit again and prove I'd be no less effective as a fighting man, some of the minor but inescapable elements of a soldier's life, like carrying heavy kit, became too difficult. My progress up the military ladder had stalled, although I fought for nearly two years to be allowed to do the course that would raise me up to full corporal. Younger men started overtaking me in rank. My hopes of a worthwhile career, of one day being a regimental sergeant-major, were pretty much screwed. Eventually, I was posted to the stores, handing out weaponry to other people so that they could go and do the things I longed to be doing. It felt like being left behind on the platform, while the train you wanted to be on had pulled out of the station.

I found myself sliding into depression. I'd long since managed to accept the fact that I'd never be David Beckham, but then I'd just cut and pasted all my hopes onto the army. So when my back problems hit, every chance of making something of myself seemed to have car-crashed. By 2009, at the age of 26, I'd had two potential careers shot from under me.

How could I go forward from here? How could I repay the faith that Mum and Dad had always had in me? In an attempt to find some focus, some direction, I decided to study for a degree in Security and Risk Management. But because I didn't have many GCSEs, I wasn't eligible to do that. So first I had to do a year-long foundation course with Leicester University, which I did in my free time. It helped. It made me feel my future wasn't entirely behind me. Of course, the big stonking issue was that the armed forces was more than just a job, more than just an escape from a crap life in some factory in the arse-end of Blackpool. As Dad had long ago found out, as most soldiers did, it got under your skin, became the heart-beat of your identity. Being a soldier was almost who you were.

Things came to a crunch when I managed to escape from the stores for a week or two. My regiment was going out to the Falkland Islands for a three-month tour of duty. Naturally I wasn't included, but I managed to wangle a flying visit as part of the logistics support team needed to make sure all the kit and weapons were in place before the arrival of our colleagues. I'd always wanted to see the islands, because Dad had been there in the war of 1982. It was a hell of a long way to go; a cold, desolate place; the edge of the world and no mistake. Empty except for thousands of sheep and vicious penguins; silent apart from the squawking of seabirds and the roar of the South Atlantic winds. Hard to believe these wild craggy landscapes had once echoed to the crash of missiles and the crackle of gunfire. I visited Mount Harriet, the scene of one of the fiercest battles of the conflict in which Dad had fought nearly 25 years earlier. At that moment he was thousands of miles away, but I'd never felt closer to him than I did right then.

Maybe it was standing on that mountain in those merciless gales that finally blew the cobwebs from my mind and helped me to see things clearly. My life as a soldier was going nowhere. Dad had moved on to other things after his life in the military. He'd recognised that a chapter in his life was over. I needed to have the balls to do the same.

The deaths in Iraq of Alan Brackenbury and Richard Shearer, both so shockingly young, would teach me that there was no time to tread water. I'd also just faced another significant death when Jon Neve, my first army mentor, was killed by a brain tumour when only in his thirties. It was a terrible loss, but part of him lives on in me and in each young soldier he ever trained.

The lesson from these three deaths was crystal clear. Anything could be waiting to explode in your face, be it an insurgent's bomb or a diagnosis of terminal illness. I wanted to take control of my life and much as I loved the army, the rigid discipline necessary in military life doesn't really allow you to do that. You're always a bit of a number. Yes sir, no sir, three bags full sir. And I didn't want to be a number any more.

From the Falklands, I flew back to the army stores in Wiltshire and it seemed even grimmer now, a bit like running a fucking corner-shop. The only glimpse of light was that on the usual lads' night out down south, I'd met a really nice local girl. Laura was very pretty, lots of fun and I knew at once she was a special person. After I'd known her for a while, I was able to let her see how miserable I was beneath the famous Wylie babe-magnet charm. At my lowest point, she was endlessly supportive and without her it would all have been a thousand times more bleak.

I plodded on because there didn't seem to be an alternative. Back home to Blackpool? And then what? Back to those same old pubs, those same old faces? A job with no prospects? A life going nowhere? The thought of it chilled my blood. Day after day, I moped around, wondering how to re-draw that map of my future which I still held in my mind.

And then late one night in the stores, the phone rang. It was an old mate from Blackpool, a former Royal Marine. Any chance I could take some urgent leave? He was putting together a security team to protect a big ship in the Middle East, but somebody had let him down and he was a man short. Did I fancy a nice fortnight in warmer climes? A short sea voyage? You bet I did. Incredibly, I managed to wangle it and rushed to pack my bags. I knew sod-all about what I was heading into, though I guessed it was going to be very different from splashing about in a pedal-boat off Blackpool beach. But I never guessed it was going to change my life forever.

CHAPTER 3

The Gold Rush

To me, a pirate was Johnny Depp as Captain Jack Sparrow. Or Captain Hook in *Peter Pan*. Or Long John Silver in *Treasure Island*. Figures from those Christmas pantomimes I got taken to as a kid in Blackpool. Parrot on the shoulder. Cutlass in hand. Tricorn hat and and 18th-century frockcoat. Big strapping blokes who shouted stuff like 'avast me hearties!', whatever the hell that meant. Certainly not a skinny African kid, in a sweaty T-shirt and grubby trainers, headphones in his ears. But those skinny kids were the pirates of the 21st century. Not remotely entertaining. In fact, no laughs at all.

But these were the enemy against whom, bizarrely, I was going to find myself fighting. For a few years, pirates were going to be at the centre of my consciousness. I would live, breathe and dream about pirates. Studying their behaviour. Trying to second-guess them. Working out how to defeat the bastards. Above all, doing my duty by the people who relied on me to protect them. I'd be a long, long way from home and from those I loved. I'd be in dangerous places whose cultures I'd struggle to understand. As a boy, I'd imagined various futures for myself, but going to sea had never been one of them. All I knew of the sea was a midsummer dip off Blackpool beach with the lads, wincing as the freezing water hit your bollocks for the first time. And that was quite enough, thank you very much.

The Gold Rush was hardly an original nickname, but it was totally accurate. The motivation of that great wave of prospectors who'd migrated to California and the Klondike in the 19th century was no different to those who headed for the Horn of Africa in the early years of the 21st to fight Somali piracy. The chance to strike it rich, to make a fast, easy buck and find yourself living the dream.

This time round, instead of travelling for long, arduous months in canvas-covered wagons, the prospectors reached El Dorado on sleek aeroplanes in no more than five or six hours. Instead of endless, back-breaking toil panning for gold in muddy riverbeds, your reward would be transferred into your bank account with pleasing speed.

Instead of being dressed in an old felt hat, filthy trousers and grubby waders, you'd probably be wearing a polo shirt by Ralph Lauren and cool combat pants from the North Face catalogue, the designer label of choice for today's action-man. And far from having a straggly unwashed beard and body odour that could strip pine, it was likely you'd be deodorised, moisturised, perfumed and gelled. The name of the game however was exactly the same. In the departure lounge at Heathrow or Manchester, waiting for their flights to the Middle East, I spotted the Gold Rush boys in a split second. A stranger might mistake them at first for a bunch of football supporters heading for an away game. The back-slapping camaraderie. The lager-drinking at 10 in the morning. That whole macho lads-on-a-spree thing. But if you looked closer, you'd soon notice the difference. There were no beer bellies here. Some were taut and lean as whippets, others built like brick shithouses, but they were all fit as proverbial fiddles. Yet it was more than that. They had a certain attitude as they lolled on the airport sofas, telling jokes or playing on their mobiles. Hard to describe exactly, but maybe just a certain quiet confidence that came from having been in the armed forces and having seen and done things that most people would never experience.

Nearly all the many thousands of men, and a few women, who went to the Horn of Africa were ex-military; nearly always from the Royal Marines or from the army. And despite the fact that this was an international crisis affecting almost every country in the world, it was the Brits who were most sought-after. Our reputation as highly trained, experienced and disciplined soldiers was second to none.

Despite our undoubted loyalty to Queen and country, we were only human. We had some loyalty to ourselves as well. And nobody ever pretended that army pay was exactly fabulous. You'd not be treating the wife to many dinners at the Ritz or cruises to Bermuda. You'd certainly not be building up a nice little nest egg to comfort you in your old age. In short, the level at which you lived your life was unlikely to ever change much, unless you won the sodding Lottery. So, when the value of the British soldier suddenly soared in this brand new marketplace, it was irresistible to many. Maybe not quite like winning the Lottery, but as close as most of us were likely to get.

Hence the Gold Rush. At one stage, guys were leaving the forces in such numbers that the Royal Marines in particular became seriously alarmed and began to warn their men against such folly. Some listened, but plenty didn't. In no time, some commercial flights to the Middle East would begin to look a bit like military transits. In the arrivals halls of Cairo, Mombasa, Dar es Salaam, Colombo and Muscat in Oman, all of which became transport 'hubs' for the dispersal of security personnel, the locals must have thought they were being invaded.

In my case of course, as I waited in the departure lounge that first time, I was actually still *in* the army. When my old friend had made that late-night phone call, I knew at once that I wanted to grab his offer. Anything to get out of the bloody stores. I'd raced across the camp towards the commanding officer's quarters. It was late, but there was a huge exercise scheduled that week and I thought he might still be working at his desk. He was a fine guy who I really admired; he'd always been sympathetic to the plight my back injury had left me in but, despite his best efforts, he hadn't been able to do anything about it. Now here was a way he could finally help.

'Okay Wylie, you can have two weeks' immediate leave,' he said. 'But on the strict understanding that I know absolutely nothing about how you plan to spend it. As far as I'm concerned, you're going home to Blackpool to watch that mob you call a football team. Is that understood?'

'Understood sir. Thank you sir.'

I could hardly contain myself. And in no time at all, I was fastening my seatbelt on the runway at Heathrow. As the plane accelerated, I felt a huge surge of optimism. The depression that had been dogging me for so long seemed to lift along with the aircraft. As the clouds that had covered northern Europe gradually melted away above the Mediterranean, that sense of a new start powered through me, quashing any nervousness I might have felt. A feeling that was bolstered by seeing the aircraft cabin half-filled with guys just like me. People whose mindset I understood before I'd even met them. The thought struck me that, even if I was going to leave the services, maybe it didn't mean I would have to abandon being a military man. Maybe I was simply joining a different sort of army. And I'm not sure why, but I had that sixth sense that something life-changing was waiting for me and I vowed that I'd make a success of it. I didn't know what it was or how I'd do it, only that I would. For Jordan Wylie, this chance was make or break.

Those Somali sods didn't know what was about to hit them.

**

At this point in time, most of us on board that plane had only the vaguest knowledge of the whys and wherefores of Somali piracy. And, even over time, plenty never really took the trouble to find out. All they knew was that this was a honey-pot and they couldn't wait to stick their fingers in it. But I wasn't one of those. If I was getting into something, I wanted to know exactly what it was.

So while I was sitting in the departure lounge waiting for the flight, I'd taken myself online. It was a real eye-opener. A story that was both fascinating and incredibly sad.

Think for a moment about what you did today, before you sat down to read this book. Got up, had breakfast, travelled to work, came home, ate dinner, watched the telly? Just like most of us do. The chances are that, throughout your day, you used, ate, drank or depended on, something that had been imported into Britain. The dressing-gown you slipped on when you got out of bed.

Your electric toothbrush. The ingredients of your shampoo or shower gel. What you had for breakfast; the muesli, the banana, the kiwi fruit. The car in which you drove to work or the fabric of your seat on the bus or train. The coffee beans that kept you going through the day. The super-screen TV you stretched out in front of afterwards. The bottle of wine you opened. The alarm clock you're going to set for tomorrow morning. The things we bring in from far corners of the planet affect us at every minute of our daily lives. And over 90 per cent of these imports reach us by sea. Amazing really, when we can send men into space and flash a selfie round the world in a split second, that we still rely on something as simple and old-fashioned as a boat to deliver so much of what we take for granted. A boat and a bunch of brave people to steer her to her destination. Just like the Greeks did, the Phoenicians, the Romans and every civilisation since the year dot.

Without merchant shipping, I realised, our lives would become unrecognisable. Economies would totter and millions of jobs would be lost. The seas cover nearly three-quarters of the earth's surface. They are the superhighways of the planet. That's why, when a threat emerges to the safety of the oceans, the consequences are serious for everyone. Such a threat, I read, emerged in the early years of this century. By spectacularly bad luck, it rose up in one of the most vital sea lanes anywhere in the world.

The Horn of Africa is a jagged tranche of land jutting out from the eastern flank of the 'dark continent' towards the countries of the Middle and Far East. For centuries, the waters around it have been an important trading route for the surrounding countries, originally just trading amongst themselves. But the opening of the Suez Canal in the late 19th century made it of massively greater importance. Now there was a far faster direct link between the east and the west and every year thousands of ships poured through the Red Sea and the Gulf of Aden; as if what had been an ordinary arterial road had been suddenly upgraded to a 10-lane highway. The Suez Canal was one of the most impactful man-made achievements of all time. It really had changed the world. The seas leading to and from it must be kept safe and secure at all costs.

There's an old saying that trouble at sea always comes from trouble on land and the countries in this region had often been highly volatile places. In the 19th and 20th centuries, the imperial powers of the west had been the big players; keen to protect their trading interests and, let's be honest, to exploit the resources of these wild, uncharted territories. But in the post-colonial age after the Second World War, when the sun finally began to set on the age-old empires, most of these countries had embraced their independence with enthusiasm. But things had often been a hell of a lot harder than they'd expected.

Among these was Somalia, the country whose long coastline contained the Horn of Africa. Once a colony dominated by the British, the Italians and the French, Somalia's road to self-determination had been as rocky as its arid, tropical landscape. For decades, there was a rumbling conflict between those who wanted to modernise the country and those who were still loyal to the ancient ways of the tribes. It finally erupted in 1991, when the president was overthrown by a coalition of the various clans and a long-running civil war broke out. Several rebel factions vied to take control and over 20,000 people were killed in the first year alone. It was a mess, a very bloody mess.

As so often happens, war brought famine in its wake. The civil unrest brought about the collapse of Somalia's agriculture which in turn led to mass starvation. The outside world sent relief, but it's reckoned that more than three quarters of the food was hijacked by tribal leaders and exchanged for weapons. It's believed that more than 300,000 starved to death and a million more suffered from malnutrition. The United Nations got involved, spearheaded by the Americans. But for the next 15 years, the bloody mess just went on and on; the opposing factions ripping the country apart like two dogs fighting over a blanket. In time, Somalia crash-dived into what is known as a 'failed state'. A society that no longer functions properly; where the rule of law has broken down, where the economy is in meltdown, where corruption and crime are flourishing and where the government has become too ineffectual to provide its people with the basic structures necessary to make peaceful daily life possible. Sometimes, a state might only 'fail' for a certain period of time, but in the sad case of Somalia, it was to be the 'new normal' for the next two decades.

From what I could see, *The New York Times* pretty much summed it all up when it called Somalia 'the most dangerous place in the world', adding that 'the whole country has become a breeding ground for warlords, pirates, kidnappers, bomb makers, fanatical Islamist insurgents, freelance gunmen and idle, angry youth with no education and way too many bullets'.

And it was to this violent corner of the globe that I and

all the others who'd so eagerly joined the Gold Rush were now heading. In our brand new North Face gear and high hopes in our hearts.

CHAPTER 4

A Toe In The Water

'Who the fuck do you think you are?' he asked.

I was stumped for an instant answer. I'd just come out of the loo and it's not the sort of thing on the tip of your tongue when you're still doing up your flies.

He glared at me, waiting for a response. He was about twice my age, old enough to be my dad, but strongly built. If it came to blows, I didn't expect to be the victor. Luckily I could see he'd had a few, so maybe if he threw a punch he'd hit the bathroom door instead.

'I'm Jordan Wylie,' I said with a smile, hoping that a cheery approach might work.

'And who the fuck does Jordan Wylie think he is?'

'Sorry?'

'What's your experience son?' he demanded. 'Why are *you* Deputy Team Leader on this job? Me and some of the other guys here are former Royal Marines or Special Forces. Why should we take orders from a donkey-walloper like *you*?'

I kept the smile fixed to my face, just to show I didn't mind the nickname which other soldiers often gave to anyone in the cavalry.

'Because that's what I've been hired to be,' I replied.

'It's a fucking joke in my opinion,' he said. 'You ever

been to sea before?'

'Not for long,' I said, visualising those pedal-boat trips back home. Since I'd never even been on a cross-Channel ferry, these were the largest 'ships' I'd yet been on.

'Jesus,' he said. 'Does your mother know that you're out?'

'I'll just have to try and convince you I'm up to the job then, won't I? If you'll give me a chance.'

He grunted and swayed off in search of another beer.

Oh dear. And I'd been having such a nice time too. We were in Doha, the capital of Qatar, at a party thrown for us in a luxurious villa owned by some big cheese in the security company who'd hired this motley crew of British squaddies. It was one amazing gaff; all glitter and gilt, straight out of James Bond. I half expected to meet a guy in an eye-patch stroking a white cat or to discover the pool was filled with piranha fish. If Daniel Craig had strolled in, I'd not have been surprised.

This time last week I'd been freezing my arse off in rain-sodden Wiltshire, now I was billeted in a five-star hotel, all expenses paid, while we waited for the ship to be ready to embark. It was very nice, lolling in the Jacuzzi, ogling the bikini-clad totty on the sun-loungers and picturing that 500 quid flying into my bank account every single day. Christ, this was the life. No more muddy army boots for me; it was flip-flops from now on.

But my confrontation with the former Royal Marine was just the first instance of an issue that would arise frequently in the future. I'd often come face to face with somebody much older who had trouble accepting me in any authority over them. It was also tied in with that old army snobbery and its sense of pecking-order. If I'd spoken with a plum in my mouth and been called Hugo, it would have been fine. But I was just a squaddie like them, a boy from Blackpool, so it wasn't.

Standing outside that bathroom door, I decided I'd damn well show him that I could do the job as well as he or his mates might. Two fingers to the lot of them. I'd once, thank God briefly, had a job at my local Tesco back home. For 12 long hours a day, my job was to raise and lower the car park barrier. It was soul-destroying, but I'd needed the money and, much as I'd hated it, I'd decided to be the best car park barrier operative who'd ever lived. And I bloody well was. I was never late, always looked smart and had a cheery smile for every Tesco customer who went in or out of that sodding car park. I knew it was all about attitude and making my contribution, however small it might be. My dad had taught me that and I was determined to apply it again here and now.

The only real reason I'd been made Deputy Team Leader of this eight-man squad was because my mate from home was in charge. He was always one for taking risks and he was taking a big one on me, so there was no way I was going to let him down. By the end of this two-week trip, I was going to make anyone who'd doubted I was up to the job admit that they were wrong.

'Jesus, look at the size of that,' said one of the guys. The rest of us just stared.

Moored at the dockside was the largest ship I'd ever seen. Her hull towered over us like a sheer cliff-face of blue-painted iron. Her name was the *Suez Cape Ann* and she was about to embark on her maiden voyage. She was a spanking new, state-of-the-art liquified natural gas (LNG) tanker, though you couldn't have called her a great beauty. Forget the sleek lines of the old sailing ships, the first steamboats or the great Transatlantic liners; the merchant ships of the 21st century were big dumpy workhorses, unconcerned about appearance. But she was certainly sensational in every other way. At a cost of over $100 million, she was over 280 metres long and more than 45 metres wide with a gross tonnage of nearly 100,000 tons. Moving at over 20 knots, she was double-hulled to prevent any leakage of her precious, and dangerous, cargo. And for the next two weeks she was going to be home.

From the fleshpots of Doha, we'd come down to the port of Balhaf in Yemen. This huge new LNG terminal had been opened only in 2006, built with over 4 billion American dollars. Brand new or not, it was a spartan industrial landscape of endless, intersecting pipelines and enormous storage tanks, made even bleaker by the expanses of black lava that rolled away from the sea up towards the crater of an extinct volcano. Security at Balhaf was tighter than a duck's arse, mostly controlled by former French Foreign Legion soldiers, a bunch of very tough cookies indeed. But that wouldn't prevent it being attacked again and again, in the years to come, by terrorist forces of all colours.

I'd soon discovered that my role on the *Suez Cape Ann* wasn't an anti-piracy mission at all, just simple counter-terrorism work in the face of a constant threat from Al Qaeda. The actual job was pretty straightforward, though it was bloody important. The ship was heading for Boston in the USA and there was enough LNG in her vast holds to provide energy to the state of Massachusetts for a fair old while.

This meant that she was, in effect, a floating bomb. If Al Qaeda or any other group had managed to get a device on board which would detonate that bomb, everything for miles around would have been blown to kingdom come. Again and again, diving teams went down to check that nothing had been attached to her hull. Her American owners were so nervous they'd hired the likes of us to make sure that catastrophe didn't happen.

'9/11' had changed everything. After that cataclysmic event, global security moved onto a totally different level. From airports, dockyards, military installations and oil and gas terminals, the need for protection would mushroom, as the atrocities continued at shopping malls, train stations, even cinemas and theatres. The new Millennium was turning out to be a darker time than anyone would have predicted.

The world was in big trouble and the source of much of it was the Middle East and Africa. From these countries, a whole network of terrorist groups had popped up like painful blisters. Al Qaeda, Al-Shabaab, Boko Haram. Correspondingly, it was the shipping-lanes in this corner of the globe which gradually became the most worrying to navigate. And when the curse of maritime piracy then appeared, it was a double whammy. It was just a lousy coincidence that these very routes were among the busiest and most vital for world trade.

Before this perfect storm blew up, security measures on most merchant ships had been almost non-existent. For decades, they'd cheerfully criss-crossed the oceans without a care in the world. By 2004, the International Maritime

Organisation, which is part of the United Nations, had issued a set of guidelines called the International Ship and Port Facility Security Code (ISPS). This was a set of basic measures, calibrated at three different levels, to protect ships, both at sea and in port. Level 1 might be having a crewman checking the identification of visitors on the gangway. Level 2 could be making sure everyone was searched. Level 3 might be denying all parties access to the vessel. It was hardly high-tech but it was a starting point and certainly better than nothing.

The most dangerous period for ship security is always in port. That's the time when so many people have valid reasons for strolling up that gangway: cargo managers, technicians, port officials, people delivering food, water, medical supplies and all the other hundred and one things a ship needs on a voyage. But if a port is a threat to the safety of a ship, it also works the other way round. A ship, especially if carrying dangerous cargo, can be a potential danger to the place in which it's moored. That's why there are always a whole bunch of local authorities who expect to come on board to check exactly who you are and what you're carrying. Considering what the *Suez Cape Ann* had in her holds, they were over us like a tramp on a plate of sausage and chips. At times, I needed 10 pairs of eyes, all going in different directions.

My job was grandly called Access Control, but merely meant that it was down to me who could get on and off this prime terrorist target. I had to have an iron fist if necessary, but it needed to be firmly inside the proverbial velvet glove. When checking the identities of people from a very different culture, courtesy and sensitivity were always vital. I always tried to employ a certain amount of the Wylie charm, while being very careful not to overstep the mark. A pleasant smile and a 'good morning' in Arabic were fine; a high-five and a cheery wink definitely weren't.

If a man approached the gangway wearing a headdress, I had to ask him to remove it in the most respectful manner I could muster. Like most British military who'd served in Iraq or Afghanistan, I'd done a course on interacting with the peoples of the Middle East, but it was easy to make a tiny, thoughtless mistake which could easily cause serious offence. For instance, trying to shake the hand of a woman would be regarded as a grave insult by her husband. There were dozens more possible gaffes like that of which you had to be constantly aware.

One part of my task was making sure stowaways didn't get on board. I discovered they could be really crafty buggers, but you had to admire their guts. Sometimes they crouched on the roofs of the containers which were being swung aboard the ship by the dockside cranes; a risky game to play. The moment the container kissed the deck they scampered off to find the nearest hiding place. I got pretty good at figuring out where these might be, though I kicked myself once when, betrayed by a sudden sneeze, I found somebody enjoying a packed lunch inside a lifeboat. I'd never thought to check there before, but it was a perfect hideout when you think about it. And if the ship was about to sink, you'd be good and ready.

'You clever little sod,' I said.

I did a 12-hour day; six hours on, six hours off, then the same again. The free time wasn't long enough to do much else but sleep, eat, have a shower and watch a movie. There was nothing much around the port area that tempted you to explore ashore. It was a shame in a way that my very first job was on a ship like this one, because she spoiled me for ever after. The LNG industry was a very lucrative one and no expense had been spared to make her ultra-luxurious. As always in modern ships, the living accommodation was in a superstructure that rose from the aft of the ship; a bit like a three or four-storey apartment block.

'Jeez, have you seen what's inside this cabin?' said one of my team when we'd explored on the first day. 'There's a fucking Jacuzzi in here!'

And there was. There was also a swish restaurant, a gym and a small cinema. All this and 500 quid a day too. We could hardly believe it.

For the next few years, I was to spend my working life inside these superstructures. Whether luxurious or crappy, spacious or cramped, they were all essentially the same. It was a world of narrow passageways, iron staircases with steep gradients, crew lounges with blokes sprawled around watching DVDs or playing computer games, dining rooms that never quite lost the faint smell of cooking and cabins that carried the even stronger whiff of sweaty blokes.

'For Christ's sake Dave, will you change those fucking socks!' was often heard echoing along the passageways.

I was well-used to the less appealing aspects of communal living but, below decks at least, the maritime life would always be more claustrophobic than an army barracks and it would take time to adjust to that. And always there was the background hum of the engines and the sense of the floor shifting under your feet. But there would be compensations; the climate, the beauty of the open seas, the glimpses of dolphins and whales cresting the waves in the sunshine. You didn't get much of that in Wiltshire. The world of the ship was a world unlike any other; many challenges, but many charms too.

Eventually the *Suez Cape Ann*, fluttering with flags and bunting for her maiden voyage, slipped her moorings and let the tugs nudge her out of Balhaf harbour. Once we were out at sea, I didn't have a lot to do. Now we'd left the dangers of the docks behind us, there seemed to be an attitude that we were reasonably safe. In retrospect, this now seems incredible. By this point in 2010, there had been plenty of pirate attacks, including the notorious case of the *Sirius Star* and the assault on the *Maersk Alabama* (the story of which was told in the 2013 movie *Captain Phillips*). But the international community, though it had by now sat up and taken notice, was still in the early stages of a concerted response.

The owners of the *Suez Cape Ann* wanted our team on board to protect her through the risky sea-lanes leading towards the Suez Canal, but then we'd disembark and she'd carry on alone across the Med and the Atlantic to her ultimate destination. But apart from us, on the ship there were none of the other basic protection measures that would very soon become standard. Perhaps, it was felt that the *Suez Cape Ann* was simply too massive to fall prey to something as tiddly as a few scrawny kids in a pirate skiff. It wouldn't be long before that attitude would be widely considered bonkers.

I just got on and did the job as best I could. Whenever, as second in command, I had to give an order to any of these older guys, I did it politely but firmly, leaving no doubt that I expected it to be obeyed. If any raspberries were blown behind my back, I never heard them. Over the two weeks,

I took it all very seriously indeed, much more so than some of the others who seemed to view this job as a walk in the park compared to the scenarios they'd had to deal with in Iraq or Afghanistan. I guess some of them felt they'd proved themselves already and could just coast along. I was exactly the opposite. I still felt that I'd proved next to nothing at all and that feeling drove me on, colouring almost everything I did. I was going to make my mark and it seems that it worked.

Just before we disembarked in Egypt, somebody came up to me with a hand outstretched. It was the guy who'd accosted me outside that bathroom door.

'You've done a good job Jord,' he said. 'I apologise. I'll not judge a book by its cover again.'

I was chuffed. It felt like a second passing-out parade. During the voyage, I'd discovered that he was a really great bloke who I'd grown to admire and respect. His name was Daren Knight, known to all as Daz. In the years to come, we'd become good friends and I'd learn a lot from him. These days he's a respected expert on global security issues but, whenever we meet for a pint, I still enjoy reminding him of when we each thought the other was a twat.

When I watched the ship move out of the port without me, it almost hurt. But now at least I knew where my future lay. I'd been offered a year's contract with the security company, working two weeks a month, a fortnight on, a fortnight off. I was gagging to accept it there and then, but I needed to remember I was still in the army.

I stayed briefly in another five-star hotel, had one last dip in a sun-drenched swimming pool, then flew home. All expenses paid.

Now of course I had to return to camp. So it was back to the fucking stores and what a culture shock that was. Grey skies and pelting it down. As I carried out the usual tedious duties, I couldn't stop thinking of that villa in Qatar, the posh hotels and the wide open waters of the Gulf of Aden. I ached to get back there. There had to be a way.

But there was one big difference in me after that fortnight. The depression had vanished. I'd got my drive and passion back. Everyone saw it. Laura was amazed by how much I'd altered in so short a time; she'd never really known the 'old me'. She was pregnant by now and the baby was imminent. In November 2009, the life of Evie Grace Wylie began. 'Wow' doesn't even begin to cover it. And it felt that the life of the bloke she'd have to call Dad might be starting again too, because the colonel noticed the change in me. He must have pulled a few strings or called in some favours but, by some miracle, he managed to get me out of the army in just a few weeks. Like queuing for a bus, you wait for ages for a bit of happiness then two come along at once.

The only tiny cloud on my new, bright blue horizon was that nagging awareness of the tainted reputation that private security companies had, partly at least, brought on themselves. It troubled me a bit and, as always, I turned to Dad for advice. When his own military career had come to an end, he'd gone into the private security sector, too. I'd noticed it was something he rarely talked about; just the odd snippet over the years. He'd once told me that he'd found himself having to mix with some dodgy characters on missions that were equally dubious and easily deniable by any government if they were discovered to have taken place. He'd got himself out of it as soon as he could. So was that a bad omen for me then? Despite the gloom of the last year or so, I was still fiercely proud of the time I'd spent in the army and the small contribution I'd made to my country. Dosh or no dosh, I didn't want to move into a field that was morally suspect.

But my parents didn't try to dissuade me. They'd seen all too clearly how miserable I'd been and were excited that I might have found a new direction. Dad advised me to make a clean break from the army and not look back with any sort of regret. Besides, fighting against piracy, protecting ships and the innocent people, seemed to him like a decent way to make a living.

'Go for it' was the gist of his advice. 'But keep yourself above reproach. Never drop your standards. Always remember you were a soldier in the King's Royal Hussars. In some ways, you always will be. Live up to that.'

He still felt however that I shouldn't put all my eggs into one basket. Security work wasn't always secure. Who knew how long this pirate caper would last? Was it a storm in a teacup that would blow over inside a year, two at the most? Then where would I be? Back home, looking for a job, that's where.

So even though I now had the maritime security contract in my pocket, Dad said I needed something else to fall back on. As soon as I'd formally got out of the army, he paid for me to do a quick course in close protection work. Unbelievably, I was hired to drive Alan Hansen, the footballer and TV pundit to a dinner at the Dorchester Hotel. But the satnav seemed to be having a nervous breakdown that night and, not knowing London at all, what should have been a 10-minute journey ended up taking about 45.

Luckily, Hansen had a sense of humour. I came to the con-clusion that it wasn't a life I was cut out for.

Anyway, the path to my future now seemed clear. I kept my suitcase nearby, my polo shirts and smart combat pants washed and ironed, ready to move fast when the next call came from my mate. I could hardly wait. And I kept remembering the last conversation I'd had with him as I'd left the *Suez Cape Ann*.

'Good lad, Jord,' he'd said. 'You passed the test.'

'Yeah? What was that exactly?' I asked.

'I wanted to see how you coped on a ship,' he said. 'I needed to know if you could handle the life.'

'Why, what have you got in mind?'

'A lot more than poncing about catching stowaways and frisking under a few *djellabahs*,' he replied. 'This trip was just your dress rehearsal, mate.'

'For what?'

'For the pirates, mate,' he said. 'It's time for you to take on the pirates.'

CHAPTER 5

Pirate Alley

The piracy I was now going to fight against was just one of the symptoms of Somalia's catastrophe, but it was to be the one that grabbed headlines all round the world. With its impact on international trade, this violent storm in a foreign tea-cup really was going to matter.

Yet those headlines had been a long time coming. It wasn't until around 2008 that piracy off the Horn of Africa became a serious phenomenon. That was 17 long years after the beginning of the Somali civil war. So why had it taken so long for this new threat to explode?

Somali piracy, at least in its early stages, was born of deprivation and hopelessness. You lived in a country that had become a frightening place. You couldn't get a decent job. You struggled to get enough to eat. Your future, if you had one at all, was pretty fucking bleak. So you were a bit scared. You were also getting angry. Because, as Somalia had gradually sunk to its knees, others had taken advantage of its weakness and descended on it like vultures.

The fishing industry was a source of both employment and, obviously, desperately needed food. But in the early years of the new Millennium, illegal fishing fleets, mostly from the Far East, increasingly began to plunder Somali waters. Not just stealing their vital stocks of fish, but ripping up the precious coral reefs and wrecking livelihoods for decades to come. And just as destructive as what was taken out of the waters was what was put *into* them. Somalia's seas had become a favourite rubbish tip for foreign companies to dump their toxic waste. The extent of this became shockingly apparent after the terrible tsunami of 2004 when the great wave disgorged huge amounts of toxic material onto Somalia's beaches. It's estimated that thousands of people died as a result.

So, to the average Somali, not only was his country ripping itself apart internally, it was now being attacked from the outside. Fear and anger are a powerful combination and it's no wonder, so many got the urge to fight back. By 2008, this dire situation coincided with the government of Puntland, the northern region of Somalia at the tip of the Horn of Africa, being no longer able to pay the wages of its security forces. Suddenly, large numbers of policemen and soldiers were desperate to find other work and plenty soon joined the disgruntled fishermen. If you had a gun and enough guts, why not? It was better than starving or wasting your days lying in the shade chewing *khat* leaves and turning into a zombie.

And that's when Somali piracy really began. Up till this point, it had usually been just a bunch of guys in a trawler sailing just a few miles out to fire their guns, steal some phones and laptops and scare the bastards so they didn't come back. In short, the sea-going equivalent of a mugging. Anyway, what cause could possibly be more just? They didn't see themselves as pirates at all; they were the 'coast-guards' and even 'saviours' of Somalia. There was a definite whiff of Robin Hood about the whole carry-on. But then the mood slowly changed. They saw how easy it could be to attack even quite a sizeable ship. Their ambitions and, quite literally, their horizons broadened. The phenomenon which had been simmering gently for several years, now suddenly boiled over.

For most of that time, the rest of the world hadn't been too worried. After all, there had been piracy in these waters for 2,000 years. From the Ancient Greeks to Victorian explorers like Sir Richard Burton, a passage around the Horn of Africa had always been recognised as a dodgy undertaking. But by 2008, the international community realised there might be a big problem to be dealt with. That year alone, there had been over 20 serious attacks, hostages taken, big ransoms demanded.

Arguably, what made the world really sit up and take notice was the stupendous hijacking in November 2008 of the *Sirius Star*, a massive Saudi Arabian oil tanker. She was 330 metres long and weighed 318,000 tons. She carried $100 million worth of oil; about 2 million barrels, which represented no less than a quarter of the total daily output of Saudi Arabia's wells. Had her violent capture led to a major oil spill, it could have been an even worse environmental disaster than the *Exxon Valdez* incident in 1989, and wrecked the ecosystems of the Indian Ocean. Ships didn't come much bigger, more valuable or more dangerous than the *Sirius Star*.

What's more, it had been attacked over 800 kilometres off the coast of Kenya, way beyond Somalia's own fishing-grounds. This shattered the previous cosy belief that most pirates were opportunistic chancers, who never strayed far from their own coastline. To track down the *Sirius Star*, the pirates had had to sail at least three days out from land. They'd used an old fishing trawler, a *dhow*, as a 'mothership' and, having found the tanker, launched their small attack skiffs from there. In other words, the whole thing had been cleverly and meticulously planned. Armed to the teeth, they'd swarmed over this massive ship and taken control of her in next to no time. Then they'd forced her crew to sail to an anchorage off the northern coast of Somalia and demanded a ransom of $25 million to be delivered within 10 days.

The world's naval forces, the international shipping companies, their insurers and of course their captains and crews were gobsmacked. Nobody could quite believe it. Naturally, the predominant response was outrage, but there was also some grudging respect for the sheer effrontery of the brigands. Reading about it in the papers, I remember thinking 'wow, that took balls.'

The negotiations to free the *Sirius Star* lasted two months, the pirates eventually settling for $3 million. Luckily no hostages were harmed but what took a very hard knock was international confidence in the security of merchant shipping. In the turbulent wake of the hijack, the price of oil briefly rose on the world's markets.

So, was this just an awesome one-off or the shape of things to come? The answer arrived pretty fast. The attacks, big and small, kept on happening. At roughly the same time as the *Sirius Star* hijacking, a smaller Ukrainian vessel the *Faina* was seized. This time the negotiations to free the crew took five months. And this time, somebody did die; the captain had a stroke due to the stress of events.

The irony lay in the *Faina* cargo: 33 armoured tanks, 150 grenade launchers, six anti-aircraft guns and enough ammunition to blow every pirate in the Horn of Africa sky-high. But, locked tightly away in the hold, it did them no good whatsoever.

By now, the international community could see that Somalia's fragile government could do next to nothing to police its own coastline and put a stop to all this. Sporadic attempts had certainly been made, but they were blighted by both a lack of resources and the whiff of corruption. It was crystal clear that international shipping would have to do the job itself. So everybody got together at the United Nations to figure out how that could be achieved.

It was going to be bloody difficult, that was for sure. About two million square miles of sea were involved. Around 25,000 commercial ships a year needed to pass through these now dangerous waters. The obvious answer was to deploy the world's naval forces against this new enemy, but most of these had a long list of other things to do as well; together they could commit no more than about 30 of their ships to the Somali crisis. One commentator succinctly said it was like trying to police the whole of Europe with only eight police cars.

Despite this lack of resources, the international navies did their very best to patrol what became formally known as the High Risk Area and soon to everybody else as 'Pirate Alley'. State-of-the- art warships were manned by the sailors of several nations; expert, disciplined and committed, but it just wasn't enough. They needed to be in the right place at the right time. Often, by the time the 'police car' got to the scene of the crime, it was just too late. That these forces were simply unable to be the magical solution to Somali piracy soon became all too apparent. Something else was needed, and fast. And it was pretty obvious what that was. The targeted ships would have to protect themselves. Every time, they sailed into Pirate Alley, they'd have to be ready to retaliate. Fast and hard. Their lives might depend on it.

But the seafarers of the merchant navies were just that. They were sailors, engineers, stokers, cooks. Most of them had never held a gun and never wanted to. It was clear that a new type of crew member was needed to join the ranks. One who had the skills to fight back against the pirates of Somalia, to keep the ship and her valuable cargo safe. But there was much more to this than assets and balance sheets. This was about keeping people out of danger. As Somali piracy tightened its grip in the years after 2008, there would be many tragic tales.

So whoever could help guard the world's seafarers against this awful new threat to their lives and livelihoods would be doing a worthwhile job. To my surprise, I was to find myself one of this new breed of crewman.

Once I'd joined the Gold Rush, friends back home would often ask, in disbelief, how the hell a relatively small number of men could possibly board and seize control of a bloody great ship and hold it to ransom? It seemed ridiculous, quite inexplicable. For instance, the *Maersk Alabama*, the ship in the *Captain Phillips* movie, had been assaulted by no more than four pirates. Suddenly it was under the control of a bunch of trigger-happy guys, many of them little more than boys, with no more idea how to navigate a complex vessel than fly to the moon.

There was no easy, neatly packaged answer to that question. In fact, there was often a whole sheaf of reasons why a ship would fall prey to attack and hijacking. But in that question there was often a fundamental error of perception - that a large ship was a thing of strength and invulnerability. The truth was often the very opposite.

Those long night-shifts I put in on the bridge-wing brought that frailty home to me. On my first few trips, I wondered if I could handle that powerful awareness of our isolation. A merchant ship at sea is a lonely object. Perhaps hundreds of miles from land. Even in relatively busy waters, it is quite possible not to see another vessel for days on end. Today's gigantic container ships and tankers are often crewed by no more than 15 or 20 men. And regardless of advances in the art of ship-building, the sea can be a harsh mistress, suddenly deciding to toss you around like a cork. Even if you've got that Jacuzzi, gym and five-star cuisine, it can still be hell out there. On my second trip, we hit rough weather. The five-star cuisine in my stomach soon went over the side, quickly followed by any desire to live. I tried hard to butch up and get on with the job, but the old salts on board didn't make that any easier.

'Bacon sandwich, Jord?' somebody would laugh as they went past you and you'd retch for the hundredth time, your stomach muscles tied in knots.

Thankfully, it isn't quite as lonely as in days of old. The revolution of modern satellite technology means the ship can communicate with land far more easily in an emergency such as an engineering problem or serious illness. Help can be summoned at once, even if it might take a fair old while to reach the vessel. At all times, somebody somewhere will know roughly where the ship is located. Unfortunately, this no longer means just maritime rescue organisations. In the time it takes to boil a kettle, everyone and his granny can now go online and find out, pretty accurately, where any merchant ship may be. And that of course includes the bad guys. It was the easiest thing in the world for the Somali pirate gangs to sit under a shady tree, hunched over their laptops, and choose exactly which tasty prey they were going to hunt down.

Above all, it was the sheer size of modern merchant vessels which was to make them such an easy target. The largest of the new 21st century ships were now dubbed 'post-Panamax', i.e. too big to go through the Panama Canal (though not Suez). Over 300 metres, when fully loaded, they might weigh as much as 300 jumbo jets. Their rudders were the size of a double-decker bus. They could rarely travel faster than 20 knots, whilst oil tankers would rarely exceed 15 knots because of the volatility of their cargo. It would need four or five miles to bring them to a halt and even longer to turn around. In short, they were gentle giants whose responses were slow and lumbering. All of this was good news for anyone who wanted to attack them.

The skiffs used by the Somali pirates were just the opposite. Basically just inflatables driven by powerful outboard engines, they could outrun almost any merchant ship. Their small size but high speed meant they were nimble too, able to duck and weave and outmanoeuvre almost any stratagem the ship might adopt to escape. If the attack took place fairly close to land, the skiffs might operate on their own. For operations far out at sea, they would be attached to a mother-ship; often a fishing-boat which had itself been hijacked and which was big enough to provide accommodation and storage for weapons. From this mothership, the skiffs would go out on their daily hunting expeditions. Bristling with automatic weapons and rocket propelled grenades. Ready for anything.

That's not to say that cornering a big ship was a piece of cake. Not even in the early days of the phenomenon, before ships took protective measures and then, later on, hired guards like me to protect them. Even when a ship was highly vulnerable, getting on board was still a dodgy business. If pirates were lucky, the targeted vessel might have a particularly low freeboard; the point on the ship's deck which was nearest to the water. This was nearly always at the stern, sometimes just a few metres above the waves, so that any fit young pirate could more or less leap aboard.

But if the freeboard was too high to provide easy access, the essential tool was a long rope-ladder with a grappling hook attached, which had to be thrown up and latched onto the railings around the deck. A bit like a cowboy trying to lasso a horse. Not easy, when both the skiff and the ship are moving and the swell may be rough. If the pirate succeeded, he then had to make the leap from the skiff onto the rope-ladder and climb up the vertiginous hull. This could be much trickier than it sounds. As Somali piracy gradually became more organised, the pirates were given training in such things. But many of them were young lads from inland Somalia who'd never been to sea before and who couldn't even swim. In those first years many drowned, perhaps, horribly, chopped into mincemeat by the propellers of the ship. Yet for most of these kids, and some were no more than 15 or 16, the risk-versus-reward still made piracy a highly attractive choice of career. After all, they had bugger-all future back on land.

If the pirates managed to reach the decks, the captain and crew of that ship knew they were in serious shit. At this stage, the assault was merely called an 'illegal boarding', not yet a formal 'hijack'. It would only merit that description once the pirates had wrestled control and were the guys giving the orders. But from this point on, the battle for control began. At all costs, the crew had to make sure that they were the victors. In the early years, without security guards on board, they rarely were.

It took the international community a while to fully wake up to the threat posed by piracy off the Horn of Africa. Incidents like the *Maersk Alabama*, the *Sirius Star* and a growing number of attacks on other huge and awesomely valuable ships finally kick-started some sort of integrated response. On one day alone, which become known as Black Thursday, different pirate gangs assaulted and hijacked no less than three merchant ships in the same small area and held their crews to ransom. In 2008, 84 pirate attacks were reported. By 2010, it had soared to over 180. Not all attacks were translated into successful hijacks but, in 2010, the pirates captured over 50 vessels.

In the swanky offices of the shipping companies, smart-suited executives and the anxious representatives of their insurance companies sat grim-faced with their knickers well and truly in a twist. These blokes, often graduates of posh business schools with sod-all knowledge of the realities of life at sea, tried to come up with some solutions. And fast. Out of a spectacular $7 billion total*, the shipping industry and its insurers bore about 80 per cent of the burden (the rest was represented by costs to the military). The pirates were putting them to the lash and they were beginning to bleed really hard. Those costs could be broken down into several different strokes of the lash. Insurance premiums accounted for $635 million. Thwack! The re-routing of ships away from Pirate Alley, either by hugging the west coasts of India and Pakistan or, even more costly, by going round the Cape of Good Hope, was $583 million. Thwack. Increasing the speed of vessels to outrun the pirates, though often unsuccessful, was a whopping $2713 million. Thwack.

In contrast, the amount paid out in ransoms for a hijacked ship and crew was 'only' $160 million, almost paltry by comparison but, in human terms, by far the most important. In 2011 alone, 1,180 seafarers had been taken hostage, of whom 24 had died. Nobody made jokes about Captain Jack Sparrow any more.

I learnt on my earliest trips that the first moves in the fightback were to adopt simple, easily installed measures to make the ships less like sitting ducks and increase their chances of deterring any attack. The International Maritime Organisation (IMO), responsible for setting standards and creating regulations to ensure the safety of the world's shipping, hastily laid these out in a security plan called Best Management Practices. Known to all and sundry as BMP4, this plan was to become the 'bible' for the captains of merchant ships and for security teams over the next few years and I studied it till I could quote it like some

Figures compiled by Oceans Beyond Piracy

folk can quote the good book itself. The 'commandments' in BMP4 included...

Razor-wire – great coiled labyrinths of very sharp, nasty wire, sometimes electrified, to make the pirates think twice about trying to board but, if they succeeded, to give the crew more time to get to safety.

Water-cannon – high-pressure hoses sited at intervals all around the decks, activated by remote control in the event of an attack. To swamp and destabilise the pirate skiffs, making them abort their assault or, if they begin to scale the hull, to swot them back into the sea.

Slippery paint – on the hull and on the decks.

Sonic deterrents – a long-range sonic acoustic device giving out an ear-shattering blast of sound which could be targeted, like a gun, directly onto the pirate skiffs (though pirates often got round this one by the simple expedient of wearing ear-defenders.)

The Automatic Identification System – a facility which allowed a ship to see other vessels nearby on a computer screen, identifying its name, cargo and destination. But the pirates had the technology to see this too, so the advice was to switch off the AIS when inside Pirate Alley.

But despite the glaring common sense of adopting BMP4, not all shipping companies did so, certainly not at first. Either for reasons of cost (which was a pretty daft decision considering the value of their cargoes and their vessels, not to mention the lives of their crews) or on the devil-may-care belief of 'it'll never happen to us'. To be fair, the latter response was somewhat understandable. Even at the very height of the piracy problem, a ship's chances of being attacked in Pirate Alley were still only about one in 500.

Not bad odds, unless of course you're the unlucky one. But as it became increasingly clear just how extortionate the ransoms demanded could be, many shipping insurers demanded that their clients adopt BMP4 and rewarded them for doing so with much lower premiums.

Yet Somali piracy represented far more than just a commercial problem for shipping companies and their insurers. This was a red-raw political issue too. The countries of the world simply couldn't permit one of its most important trade routes to slip under the control of gangs of sea-going muggers. Civilised societies had to hit back against such damned impertinence.

Ultimately over 30 countries around the globe would give their ships, soldiers, aircraft and equipment to combat Somali piracy. One of the first major efforts, launched in late 2008, was led by the European Union Naval Force and named *Operation Atalanta*.

Its headquarters were at Northwood, outside London, and it was under the command of some of the most distinguished generals and admirals in the game. But although it had a staff of over 1,000, its actual resources 'on the ground' were limited and variable; usually no more than three or four ships plus a couple of helicopters for reconnaissance.

To allow them to focus these resources, the International Recommended Transit Corridor was created. This was a sort of nautical safe-highway through Pirate Alley; 800 miles long, one lane in each direction with a 'central reservation' a few hundred metres wide. Merchant ships were encouraged to use the IRTC whenever possible, ideally bunched together in convoys, so making it possible for the stretched naval forces to offer them collective protection.

As further back-up, *Operation Atalanta* set up a 24/7 online service to monitor all vessels travelling through dangerous waters, to keep commercial shipping abreast of the latest piracy hotspots and to give guidance on the latest strategies to keep themselves safe.

But despite an admirable string of successes in freeing hijacked ships and their crews, all this just wasn't enough. As the pirate attacks increased in number and spread further and further from their own shores, Pirate Alley grew ever larger in size, which made countermeasures even more difficult to apply.

Following hot on the heels of the EU's initiative, the biggest boy in the playground got involved. In 2009, the USA spearheaded the formation of a new multinational naval force. Formed with a mandate from the United Nations Security Council and christened *Combined Task Force 151*, it boasted six patrol ships from the USA, the UK, Australia, Pakistan, Turkey and South Korea as well as a few patrol helicopters. Under the rotating command of some very prestigious naval leaders, *Combined Task Force 151* notched up an impressive score of successes but, as pirate activity continued to soar, it faced the same basic handicaps as *Operation Atalanta*. Too much sea, not enough resources. The impossibility of always being in the right place at the right time.

NATO also made its own contribution under the name of *Operation Ocean Shield*, charged in particular with protecting ships carrying humanitarian aid, food and other supplies, to third world countries in desperate need of it, not least Somalia itself.

Part of the international community's response to the

crisis was to liaise as closely as possible with the authorities in Somalia. After all, it was the crippled condition of that country which was the root cause of the whole problem. To give it credit, the Somali government had asked the United Nations for help to fight piracy several years back and their own small naval forces had made some feeble attempts to nip it in the bud, but these had been dogged by incompetence and the suspicion of corruption and had gradually withered on the vine. Anyway, the Somali government was a fragile edifice which could come crashing down at any time. They had more than enough on their hands coping with the bad stuff on land, never mind at sea.

Obviously, the work of *Operation Atalanta* and *Operation Ocean Shield* and of *Combined Task Force 151* tended to overlap somewhat, but who cared when, excuse the expression, the situation required all hands on deck. I have huge respect for the combined efforts of the various international navies. Without them, the whole phenomenon of Somali piracy would have been a whole lot worse and more lives lost. But nobody was more aware than they themselves about the limits of what they could achieve.

Vice Admiral Bill Gortney of the US Navy, who had launched *Combined Task Force 151*, said clearly that the 'efforts of coalition and international navies won't solve the problem of piracy.' A blunt statement which obviously begged the question…' so what the hell will?'

If you've read this far, you'll have guessed the answer to that. Yet how odd it is that, even now, some commentators writing about this phenomenon still seem reluctant to fully acknowledge the role of that third piece of the jigsaw in tipping the balance and winning the war.

And why is that? The answer is simple. Because nobody really wanted us.

When I wasn't actively engaged in the job itself, I spent as much time as I could just learning about life on board a ship. As soon as possible, I tried to stop being a dickhead landlubber who referred to the galley as the kitchen, the heads as the loos and the bow and stern as the front and the back.

I also grabbed the chance to learn some specifically seafaring skills. How to put on a life-vest. And how to launch a lifeboat. I'd always thought of those as big open inflatables, like the craft the RNLI used back home. But on huge container ships, they were more like space-pods, totally enclosed by a hard top to protect the occupants from sea and wind. Carefully equipped with rations, fresh water, medical supplies and distress flares, they were held on deck by davits which could lower them swiftly into the water or, in more advanced vessels, at the top of a chute down which the lifeboat could be propelled like shit off a shovel onto the waves. I always prayed I'd never need to be inside one of those.

I also learned a few tricks of the trade from team members who were former Royal Marines and knew far more about life on the ocean wave than I did. Such as how to shoot from a moving, unstable ship down onto a moving target, taking into account the prevailing wind conditions. Not an easy ask.

It never failed to amaze me that even the largest of the merchant ships were crewed by such a small number of people; an aircraft carrier of a comparable size might have had 1,000 men on board. Above decks, they were impressive enough, but down below was just as gob-smacking. Engine-rooms could be as big as cathedrals; several storeys high, their levels accessed by steep staircases that flew up and down like on a snakes and ladders board. The dull throb of the massive engines never stopped 24/7 and became the comforting background hum of my daily life. The engine control-room alone often looked like something out of a sci-fi movie; row upon row of flashing lights, screens, dials, levers, buttons and knobs.

This then was the strange world in which I now lived and worked. These floating workhorses ploughing their way across the sea, carrying the cargoes that people needed in every town and village across the planet. Till the turn of the Millennium, the worst worry on any voyage had been a violent storm or a refrigeration unit that packed in, turning 100,000 frozen prawns into a rotting, stinking mess. But now they were under threat as never before. It was my job to make sure everyone on board this ship reached their destination safely. And that included the prawns.

CHAPTER 6

Middle East or Wild West?

He always wore a T-shirt with the word 'paratrooper' emblazoned proudly on the front, so I made the obvious assumption. It had been quite a tense transit through Pirate Alley; an upsurge of recent attacks had made us all extra jumpy. So though I'd been working alongside this guy for the past two weeks, there hadn't been much time for small talk. It was only at the end of the job, when port was almost in sight, that I got round to asking him, soldier to soldier like, how long he'd been in the regiment.

'What d'you mean mate?'

'How long were you in the Paras?' I asked again, pointing to the ubiquitous T-shirt.

'Oh no mate,' he laughed. 'I got this T-shirt from my brother-in-law. He was in the Paras, not me.'

'So how did you end up as a guard on here ?' I asked.

He said he'd been working at the house of the operations manager of the American security company. One day he'd mentioned that he enjoyed a bit of shooting and the man had instantly offered him a security job on this voyage.

'So you know your way around guns then?' I said.

'Oh, I wouldn't say that.'

'No?'

'I've only ever shot clay pigeons and tin cans.'

I gulped.

'So what exactly is your line of work back home?' I asked.

'I'm a painter and decorator mate,' he replied. 'Been doing it for 20 years now, so this has been a nice little break.'

I gulped again. For the past two weeks, one person in the four-man team hired to protect a ship and cargo worth tens of millions of dollars had been a fucking paper-hanger. For the hundredth time, I asked myself the question that had come into my head during my first few months as a maritime security guard. Was this the Middle East or the Wild West?'

This industry had gone from being virtually non-existent to a mammoth business in just a couple of years but, as yet, it had almost no governance, no structures or licences. Having just left the rock-solid disciplines of the British Army, I was amazed. It was a rude awakening.

Basically, anybody could set up a Private Maritime Security Company (PMSC) and that's exactly what happened. Pretty much anybody did and a large proportion of them were British. Many of the first PMSCs were no more than ex-military guys sitting in a back bedroom with a laptop and a data-base of old mates. They'd set up a poncy website and a postal address in Mayfair to give themselves a bit of gloss but, more often than not, they were actually in Scunthorpe or Doncaster, with their wife cooking the kids' tea down in the kitchen.

Although, at the beginning of the Gold Rush, it was British ex-military men who were the most sought after by PMSCs, especially Royal Marines, ex-policemen were big favourites too. But such was the demand that the PMSCs weren't averse to slipping in a fair number of seriously under-qualified people. Maybe my painter and decorator was an extreme example, but there were lots of guys who really weren't fit for purpose, who'd never held a weapon in their lives, which in some cases was just as well. Often they were gym bunnies, built like tanks, shaven-headed and coming across like hard men. Usually, that image was enough to instill confidence in the client. But God knows how they'd have behaved in the face of a pirate attack. Some might have been fine, but plenty might have run screaming for their mummies.

In my first few months, it wasn't just underqualified team members who might prove a problem. When you accepted a job in good faith, there were other reasons why you could find yourself in what might well become serious shit. Four of us once arrived in Mozambique to protect a tanker on a three-week voyage to Karachi in Pakistan and back again. Only when we got to the port did we discover that we'd be unarmed. It was a last-minute gig; a big rush for the ship to embark and get on its way. In the shipping industry, every day a ship wasn't at sea meant a loss of income. There was next to no time to do a proper risk assessment of the vessel, but it was obvious at first glance that it hadn't taken even the basic BMP4 measures like razor-wire around the decks. There was certainly no possibility of doing any crew training before we sailed. And there had just been a sharp spike in pirate attacks in the waters we'd be crossing. People were particularly jittery. To travel unarmed in these particular circumstances seemed nuts.

'We're not doing it, Jord,' two of my guys said at once. 'It's suicidal.'

I got on the phone to London fast. I could feel my arm being twisted from thousands of miles away. It was a major contract for my employers. This ship had to have security and our company had to provide it. No ifs, no buts. London offered to double our £300 daily rate. My two guys still refused point blank, got a cab to the airport and flew out. Neither of them actually said 'it's your funeral', but I knew they were thinking it. Actually, so was I.

That left only me and one other guy to protect this great ship through Pirate Alley; in other words, only 50 per cent of the manpower required. And without a single weapon to use in its defence. The phone line to the UK grew hotter by the minute. Eventually, London dangled a mega-carrot. A fee of £1,000 a day for a three-week trip (you work it out). So my mate and I bit the carrot and the ship sailed.

We gave the crew a very basic crash-course on what to do in the event of an attack. With the captain's agreement, we put the ship into 'lockdown', which meant that nobody went outside the superstructure, unless their duties made it vital for them to go on deck. The two of us stayed on the bridge day and night for those three weeks; one awake, one asleep on a mattress in a corner, using earplugs to protect us from the cackle of VHF radios and the constant comings and goings of the crew. It wasn't much fun. The trick was to roll yourself up into the foetal position and try and dream of that £1,000 a day.

'Jord, I'm totally cream-crackered,' my cockney mate moaned most days.

It hardly helped to be permanently tired when our senses needed to be razor-sharp. We peered at the radar screen till our eyes began to cross. Even the most harmless-looking craft that came anywhere near was presumed guilty till proved innocent.

In the end, we got to Karachi without any major scare. And then back again to Mozambique. But we'd taken a huge gamble. In retrospect, I shouldn't have done it. Nor should I ever have done it again.

Sadly, all this was typical of my first few months. Simply put, the issue was not enough guys, not enough guns. Even if the team was technically armed, that might mean just one AK-47 between four guys. Another issue was that, even if there were sufficient weapons, they'd often be guns which none of us had ever used before, an embarrassment which we'd try hard to conceal from the captain and crew, though they probably put two and two together when they saw us doing target practice with empty oil cans thrown into the sea. We certainly didn't have machine guns, bazookas, grenades or any of the other stuff you might have seen in a Hollywood blockbuster. It was never as sexy as that.

Ammunition was often in short supply too. Once, I only discovered after the ship had set sail that the only bullets we had were fakes; a bit like the bangers in the toy guns I'd had as a kid, only louder. And despite raking it in, some PMSCs could be pretty lax about paying the guards who they'd sent into danger woefully under-protected.

But it'd be unfair to imply that all PMSCs were the back bedroom boys. There were plenty of well-established, very respectable security firms who, from the turn of the Millennium or earlier, had built up fine reputations for their land-based operations and this was the calibre of work I tried to get. So the field was getting pretty crowded.

As time went on, the industry began to regulate itself a

little more. This previously 'seat of the pants' business began to realise that offering its customers reassurances about the personnel they supplied could be an advantage in an increasingly crowded marketplace. It was no longer enough to brag that all your guards were Brit ex-military; you now needed to prove that they were also trained for maritime work. So any potential security guard had to produce a firearms certificate, a safety-training certificate, a medical certificate. He'd have to know how to put on a life-jacket, how to put out a fire on board and be able to deal with a dozen other issues he'd never have encountered in the deserts of Iraq. Soon a handful of self-made regulatory bodies sprung up with the purpose of vetting security companies on behalf of ship owners. But all this began to get a bit confusing for the merchant navy; so many different logos, so many certificates. So the International Maritime Organisation had to start advising on how to spot the respectable PMSCs from the slightly less reliable ones. It wasn't exactly foolproof but it was a step in the right direction.

Despite all this, it would rarely be possible for me to pick and choose the men on my teams like chocolates from a box. It would often just depend on who was available and in the area. The final selection would usually be made in the 'operations room' of the PMSC back in the UK. On the occasions when I did have an input, I'd always try to put together a squad with a variety of specialist skills. A practical engineering type who'd be good at erecting razor-wire, fortifying doors and windows. A whizz-kid with satellites, radio and other communications. A good team medic; every trained soldier has some knowledge of first aid, but some developed these skills further and were always sought-after by security companies.

Of course it was good to have old army mates appear on the team, but that could be a double-edged sword. On the plus side, there was already a 'shorthand' between you; you knew how each other operated, what the strengths and weaknesses were. On the negative side, having old pals under you could be a risk to your authority if you were the leader. Liberties could be taken, although the daily reality was that, working on a shift basis, you might hardly see each other apart from when you handed over. It would only be in the event of attack that the team dynamic might make or break your response.

In fact, as time passed, I realised that younger men who'd only recently left the forces could be better bets than the older, decorated veterans of Iraq and Afghanistan. Often they were more disciplined, hadn't yet learnt too many 'bad habits' and could be moulded a lot more easily into first-rate maritime guards than the 'old Rambos' who could sometimes be arrogant and inflexible. Shell Oil even began to stipulate these younger men when hiring its security teams, much to the disbelief and total disgust of the veterans.

Whether young or not, men who'd seen action in war zones sometimes brought big problems in their suitcases. Post-traumatic stress disorder (PTSD) often hadn't been diagnosed by any doctor or was kept secret by the men themselves in order to get through the medical for private security work. Now and again, this could have tragic results. One ex-para with PTSD, working in Iraq for the Armor security group, got drunk one night, shot two of his colleagues dead and is now serving 20 years in an Iraqi jail. So there were more than a few damaged guys out there. And sometimes, I'd find myself walking up the gangway of a ship alongside them, without knowing anything about it.

It was like *Butch Cassidy and The Sundance Kid*. That famous scene when Paul Newman and Robert Redford take a run and leap off the cliff into the river to escape the baddies.

One day in 2008, on a ship called the *Biscaglia*, that's just what had happened to my mate Carl 'Rocky' Mason. As pirates had swarmed over the decks of this Liberian-flagged oil tanker, he and the other two guys on the security team had thrown themselves off the deck into the Gulf of Aden. Eventually, they'd been winched to safety by a German naval helicopter and taken to a French warship that had been alerted to the attack.

Cue laughter and mockery. The image of tough British ex-squaddies turning tail and jumping into the drink earned its fair share of jokes. But there was nothing remotely funny about it. Few men came braver than Rocky Mason. Not only was he a former Royal Marine, he'd been a stunt-man in the film industry and had done close-protection work for a long list of celebrities, diplomats and other VIPs. If Rocky had decided there was nothing for it but to jump, it had been a matter of life or death.

But 2008 was still those early days; the world only just realising the scale of the threat. The spectacular *Sirius Star* hijack had only happened a few weeks before. That ship was still in pirate hands, the hostages still captive and the ransom still unpaid when Rocky and his mates had taken their dive from the *Biscaglia*. But this latter incident was used by those who still baulked at the use of security on merchant shipping.

One newspaper wrote that 'the limitations of private security in protecting shipping from the rise of Somali piracy were cruelly exposed yesterday...'

Bollocks. The only limitations exposed by the *Biscaglia* incident were those suffered by *unarmed* private security, placed on ships without weapons to defend either themselves or the seafarers whose lives they'd been hired to protect. This was because the journey passed through jurisdictions which prohibited the carrying of lethal weapons on board.

In this case, as soon as Rocky and his team had boarded, they'd realised how vulnerable the ship was. There were few materials with which they could 'harden' her though they did their best with what they had. But it wasn't enough against a determined enemy. With bullets from AK-47s and rocket-propelled grenades whizzing past their ears, the British team had made the crew as safe as possible, but were unable to do anything more against their violent attackers. With their backs against the wall, the sea had been their only lifeline. At least in the face of the jokes and the disapproval, the boss of Rocky's PMSC showed some guts.

'Well I think they deserve a medal.'

But there was sod-all chance of that.

Of the many private security firms that emerged after 9/11, most dealt with the indispensable tasks, for which the conventional military just didn't have the resources, with impressive efficiency and sensitivity to the culture of the country. Sadly, there were a few incidents which damaged all that. A few rotten apples poisoned the whole barrel.

The most notorious of these became known as the Blackwater case. In 2007, guards employed by the large American firm of that name fired on a crowd in Baghdad, while escorting a US embassy convoy. Fourteen Iraqi civilians were killed and dozens more injured. It had started with a few ill-judged warning shots, then escalated to lethal fire and the use of stun grenades to scatter the crowd. At one point, the Blackwater guards and the Iraqi police were firing at one another. It was a total disaster, nothing less than a massacre. An unholy row blew up between Iraq and the USA. Conflicting accounts, accusations and denials filled the air. Endless investigations, including one by the FBI itself, took place. Blackwater was eventually thrown out of the country and was forced to change its now battered name. Finally, one guard was convicted of murder and three others of manslaughter; today they're all serving life sentences in an Iraqi prison. The almost-instant effect of Blackwater was that private security firms were now forever labelled as undisciplined thugs who were a threat to the safety of decent, innocent people. The media zoomed in on them and decided they were callous mercenaries.

Despite the escalation of Somali piracy, leading to the realisation that private guards were a vital piece in the security jigsaw, that nasty niff of 'mercenary' still clung to all our coat-tails. Much of the international shipping industry approached us with the greatest reluctance and a peg on their noses.

I started out full of the best intentions, so it was sad to realise that my mates and I were a medicine that few ship owners wanted to swallow, even though they knew it could be a life-saver. But it wasn't entirely tragedies like the Blackwater incident which had created this reluctance. There were other reasons, too.

Firstly, the simple cost of hiring us. The new Private Maritime Security Companies were demanding pop-star wages to supply security staff, although this issue was partially neutralised by insurers offering lower premiums to their client vessels carrying guards. Also, the expenditure on hiring protection, however much it stuck in the gullet, was still a tiny fraction of what might need to be paid out in ransom money if a ship was seized. However there were plenty of shipping companies, certainly among the smaller fry, who just kept their fingers crossed and went on sending their ships out into Pirate Alley totally 'naked'.

Secondly, and more understandably, many ship owners worried that the presence of armed guards during a pirate attack could escalate an already high-voltage situation and leave their decks awash with the blood of their own innocent crews, caught up in the middle of a gun fight. Such a catastrophe would hardly be good for the corporate image.

Many in the international naval forces such as *Combined Task Force 151*, shared this worry, at least to some extent. So did the International Maritime Organisation, which agonised for a while, then merely issued some general guidelines to ship owners and insurers about the pros and cons of using security guards, whether armed or not. Their basic message was 'it's up to you mate.'

Whether the team had weapons or not often depended under which flag the ship sailed. The nationality of a ship's owners and of its captain and crew might have precious little connection with its flag. A very high proportion of merchant ships bore a 'flag of convenience', which meant that it was legally registered in a state where the rules and regulations were a bit less restrictive than those of their native land. For example, you might have an oil tanker owned by a British company, crewed by Indians but registered in Liberia. Or conversely, a vessel with 'Liverpool' proudly emblazoned on its stern could well be owned by Russians and crewed by Filipinos.

Favourite 'flags of convenience' were Panama, The Bahamas, Liberia, the Marshall Islands in the Pacific, the Comoros Islands in the Indian Ocean and some of the Middle East countries. But big international shipping companies with a reputation to protect had to be just a bit careful. Some ships registered in these countries had been involved in practices which were less than squeaky-clean, such as smuggling and arms dealing, so the 'flags' were grouped into a White List, a Grey List and, most damned of all, a Black List. It would always be a worry to arrive at a dock, bright-eyed and bushy-tailed, then clock the name of a Black List country painted on the arse of the boat. Oh bugger.

However the 'flags' system was good news for the PMSCs. Without it, our potential market might have been much more restricted because, at this stage, some major governments, including the USA and the UK, refused to allow armed security on any ship sailing under their national flag. Consequently, some merchant ships 're-flagged' themselves in order to be able to carry armed protection. In fact, it took till 2012 before the UK and the USA gave their blessing.

To be fair though, this hesitation was understandable to

a certain extent. There were myriad rules governing the use of lethal force in the context of war on land and these would turn out to be even more tricky to apply at sea, with all the complexities of territorial versus international waters. The bottom line was that you couldn't shoot a pirate stone-cold dead just because he'd been a naughty boy and tried to scramble up the side of your ship. You had to have a really good reason that might stand up in court.

But as with any soldier in Iraq or any copper on the streets of London, the lack of a weapon to protect yourself put many guys like me into considerable danger. In all the unarmed transits I was asked to do through Pirate Alley, I'd always have to weigh up the risk-versus-reward. Just like the pirates did in fact. Was the danger to my life and limb adequately compensated for by that pop-star salary? Did all the nice things which, for the first time in my life, I was now able to buy for Laura and my mum and dad, justify taking stupid chances? Was it worth the possibility of being delivered back home in a wooden box with a pretty wreath on top?

There were plenty of people desperate to persuade me that it most certainly was. Those guys in the back bedrooms with the laptops now had so many security jobs to fill they hardly had time to take a piss. They were goggle-eyed with the zeroes on the money transfers flying into their bank accounts. There must have been a fair old number of bank managers in the small towns of Britain pleased, but slightly baffled, to see how well certain customers were suddenly doing. The seas of Pirate Alley were made of milk and honey and I was determined to grab my share. I might never have another chance as good as this.

CHAPTER 7

Flip-flops, Scabies and Egg on Toast

It wasn't an easy task. Making the jump from a small motor-launch onto a ladder trailing down the side of a huge ship which was still moving was a scary business. Bad enough if the ladder was of metal or wood; a total bummer if it were made of rope.

When security teams joined a merchant ship, it wasn't always tied up alongside a jetty with a nice gangway for you to stroll up. Quite often, it was in the middle of a churning sea with a swell that felt like the roller-coaster on Blackpool prom. You'd be ferried out to meet it at the point where it was about to enter Pirate Alley, disembarking in the same way two weeks later when it had cleared the most dangerous waters. That meant the shipping companies only needed to pay for security during the period when it was needed most. Fine for their balance sheet, but pretty rough for us. We'd all heard of plenty of accidents - lost limbs and even fatalities - especially among those macho prats who insisted on doing it in sandals or flip-flops rather than footwear that would give you a decent grip. Statistically, you were far more likely to pop your clogs when making that leap onto the rope-ladder than when fighting any pirate. You did it with your heart in your mouth, your stomach churning and your sphincter muscle tightly clenched.

'I don't think I can do it,' said Kelly-Marie to the skipper of the launch.

'Course you can love.'

'Oh Christ.'

'You'll be fine. Just take a deep breath and go for it.'

'I can't. I really can't.'

It was unusual to have a woman on the team. We were all quite used to working with women in the military, but few ex-forces women ever applied to join the Gold Rush, perhaps put off by that 'cowboy' reputation it had in the early years. But this particular job wasn't the usual anti-pirate gig. It was also a counter-terrorism one which would involve searching other women when the ship stopped in various ports. So a woman on the team was vital and this young lady had been undaunted by the challenge. Until the moment when she faced that leap.

I was up on deck with the captain of the ship. In order to pick us up, he'd slowed down to the lowest possible speed. They always hated doing that, even for half an hour. Time was money. If they didn't deliver their cargo on schedule, grumpy questions would be asked back in the posh offices of the shipping companies. It would be a black mark against the captain's name.

'What's the delay Mr Wylie?' he asked sharply.

'Not sure sir. Quite a choppy sea today,' I replied.

He and I had only just met and there was no rapport as yet. We were still these damned interlopers he'd been forced to allow entry to his little kingdom.

Even from the height of the deck, I could see the fear on this poor girl's face. She was petrified, unable to move.

'Come on, Kelly-Marie,' I shouted down, against the wind.

She gazed up at me pathetically. The guys on the launch were doing what they could to encourage her, but it was no good. The crew of the ship were now ranged along the railings, enjoying the cabaret. The captain was well grumpy by now and marched off in the direction of the bridge.

'Sort this out please, Mr Wylie,' he snapped, his temper fraying.

Shit. Not exactly a great start. Getting off on the wrong foot could affect relationships for the rest of the voyage. If only bloody Kelly-Marie could get off on any foot at all.

'Kelly-Marie,' I shouted down one more time. 'Just do it!'

It was no good. She clung to the edge of the launch like an extremely large barnacle. It looked like she'd have to go back to shore and some other woman hired in the next port. Oh dear. I headed for the bridge to speak to the captain, expecting an explosive reaction. When I got there, there was certainly an explosion, but not the sort I expected. The captain and the officers were wetting themselves with laughter. The view from the bridge was of Kelly-Marie being winched up from the launch in the basket of the crane normally used for loading baggage and supplies. As the basket swung 60 feet above the waves, her eyes were still wide with terror.

'Well done, Mr Wylie,' the captain said. 'You're obviously a man of ingenuity.'

I didn't bother to admit it hadn't been my idea, but silently thanked whoever had had the brainwave. The whole drama was in fact a blessing in disguise. Not only had tension been broken but a bloody good laugh had speeded up the bonding process. After that, we all got on just fine.

And down on the deck, Kelly-Marie clambered out of the crane-bucket, legs a bit wobbly, but with a look of sheer relief. The crew cheered and applauded as if she had been some sea-goddess who had unexpectedly landed among them. The baggage had landed.

Not all captains turned out to be pussy-cats underneath.

On my next trip, the captain had a face blasted by years of sea-breezes and tropical sunshine. It almost seemed to be carved out of stone, like the giant faces on Mount Rushmore, softened only slightly by a wild forest of grey-black beard. Though I'm a tall man, he still towered above me. He was certainly old enough to be my father and maybe not far from being my grandad. The ice-blue Russian eyes bored into me, as if somehow he knew every mistake I'd ever made and every one I was likely to make in the future. I couldn't decide if he reminded me of Sean Connery in *The Hunt For Red October* or Ivan The Terrible. Maybe a bit of both. Whatever, he was my boss for the next two weeks. Shit.

'It is not my wish that you and your men are aboard my ship, Mr Wylie,' he said in heavily-accented English. 'It is at the order of my employer.'

'I appreciate that sir,' I replied. 'We will try to be as unobtrusive as possible.'

'Please to remember that I am the master of this ship and you are under my authority at all times,' he said. 'You will take no action without first referring it to me.'

'That is fully understood sir,' I replied, standing as straight-backed as I could, just like I used to on the parade-ground. 'My team and I are professionals like yourself and your crew.'

A sort of grunting noise came out through the beard. Hard to tell if it signified complete disdain or some trace of grudging acceptance. I decided to try one of my usual ploys.

'*Mne ochen' priyatno zdes' nakhodit'sya,* ' I said.

I'd learnt it phonetically and with a lot of effort. No doubt the pronunciation was total crap. It meant that it was a great pleasure to be here. At least I bloody well hoped that was what it meant. I never totally trusted these translation websites. Who knew if I'd just called his mother the Whore of Babylon?

But I think it'd come out right because the beard gave a twitch which was just possibly the beginning of a smile.

I extended my hand which he took without much enthusiasm, turned on my heel and strode briskly off the bridge as if it were the parade-ground at the barracks in Winchester.

By this time, the 'cheesed-off captain' was a familiar character in my life. I've explained why many shipping companies were highly reluctant to allow security teams, even unarmed, on board their vessels. But that reluctance could often be as nothing compared to the feelings of the captains themselves.

So the importance of forging a good relationship between the captain and the leader of the security team couldn't be exaggerated. At all times and in every situation, he was the ultimate authority. That was the rule of the sea and it could never be forgotten. Without his approval, there was almost no action my team could take: no high-pressure hoses activated, no rocket flares set off, no warning shots fired. It was unwise even to fart without first checking with the captain. As Columbus, Drake and Nelson had once been, the 21st-century captain was still God on the ship he commanded.

Many of the masters of these large merchant ships had been at sea for decades. They'd crossed and re-crossed the Gulf of Aden and the Indian Ocean with no bother whatsoever. They knew these waters like the sun-spotted backs of their hands. The worst they'd ever had to face was a few faulty boilers or sudden appendicitis in the crew. They tended to be pretty tough nuts, especially if they'd also served in the military at some point - as the Russians and Ukrainians in particular nearly always had. Often they were at least twice my age and that old generational issue I'd had with the other members of my teams was sometimes duplicated in the captains I worked under. Few of these grizzled veterans exactly welcomed a team of British ex-squaddies being forced upon them and their crew by some wimpy desk-jockey back at head office.

So, on every ship I joined, I also embarked on a charm offensive with both the captain and the crew. Before I arrived I found out as much as possible about both the ship itself and the people I was going to be working with. I'd always try to swot up those few smarmy sentences in the captain's native language. It didn't have to be much: good morning, goodnight, please and thank you. There's an old saying that 'courtesy is the lubricant of society' and that was so true on a ship, if you wanted personal relationships to move as smoothly as the pistons in the engine-room.

I realised early on that the best parallel was that of being a guest in somebody's house. My team had been invited, albeit with mixed feelings, to share the living space of 20 or 30 people for whom the ship was home for the greater part of the year. We'd eat our meals and spend our leisure time in their company. On some of the smaller vessels, we might even have to share a cabin with one of them. To do our job properly, we'd have to slightly disrupt their usual routines and ways of doing things. I often remembered the old saying that guests are like fish; they stink after three days. And we'd be under their roof for two or three weeks at least. So my goal was to tread with a lot of sensitivity. At the end of the transit, when the team said goodbye, I wanted the captain and crew to be sad to see us go. And I'm proud to say that it often happened.

In the next few years, I'd meet a wide variety of the species; some were inspiring guys who taught me a lot and some were nightmares. In other words, just like bosses in any walk of life.

Luckily, security teams were always given the status of officers, eating in their mess as opposed to the crew's. This was a good opportunity to get to know everyone better; not just the captain but the men immediately below him. It was useful to get a clear picture of who people were and roughly what they were responsible for, so that you didn't tread on any toes. I always spent the first couple of days trying to soak up the atmosphere of this particular ship, sussing out how it ticked and how that was going to impact on the job we were here to do.

Although it varied somewhat from vessel to vessel depending on its size and the type of cargo, the rough breakdown of responsibilities was usually much the same. After the captain, the next VIP on board was the chief engineer. They were the double-act who essentially ran the show. Underneath each of those two was a distinct hierarchy.

Directly below the God-like captain was the first (or chief) officer, who might be in charge of the everyday running of the ship, cargo logistics, human resources, dangerous goods management. The second officer's duties could be navigation, communications, the general running of the bridge, management of the vital refrigeration units in the hold. The third (or junior) officer might be responsible for monitoring the weather, cargo loading procedures, dockside security and immigration clearances.

On the chief engineer's team, you'd probably have five or six men individually in charge of areas like fuel systems, electrical systems, the desalination plant (for converting seawater into drinking/cooking water), the refrigeration units and the vital fire alarm systems.

Finally, below these two teams were the ordinary seamen whose roles included general maintenance, domestic duties, docking manoeuvres, cargo supervision – and looking out for pirates.

About one million people around the world, mostly men, worked as merchant sailors. It seemed to me that they had a hard old life, separated for most of the year from their nearest and dearest. Often hundreds of miles, and a week's voyage, from the closest land. For the higher ranks at least, there was a career ladder to climb and a pretty good salary. For the lower orders though, the pay could be pretty dire; perhaps no more than 20 dollars a day. Even this was liable to tax in their home countries, yet still they sent as much as they could spare back to their families. And the work was often hard or just tedious; heavy lifting, painting the decks or the hull, chipping off rust, making ropes.

Despite the open air and the wide seas, the seafarer's life struck me as quite a shut-in, repetitive existence. But whatever rank they held, most of those I got to know wouldn't have changed it. They didn't see it as any sort of prison; on the contrary, it was often an escape from an even tougher life on land, an exhilarating chance to see other countries and cultures. The old slogan 'Join the navy and see the world' still held true in the merchant navy in the new century.

Nearly all of the crews, at least among the more skilled, spoke at least some English, which was the international language of the sea. That fact was a stroke of luck of course. Like many Brits, few of us guys were exactly expert in other people's lingo. *'Voulez-vous coucher avec moi, ce soir?'* was about the best most of us could manage.

Many of the ships carried a rag-bag of nationalities. Filipinos were perhaps the most prevalent; around one in five merchant sailors came from these sea-faring islands. Next to them in numbers were probably Russians, Ukrainians and Indians, followed by smaller numbers from all across the globe.

In addition to the pecking-order dictated by their rank on the ship, I soon noticed that there was also a subtle form of seniority based on race. This was rarely acknowledged openly, but it was definitely there. As a rough rule of thumb, men from the western nations were most looked up to. The Russians tended to regard themselves as the *crème de la crème*, looking down on everyone else. That included British security teams, which was a bit of a surprise to many men who'd served with distinction in the British military and had a strong sense of their own status. The gentle, reserved Filipinos, perhaps just because they were so numerous at sea, were often at the bottom of the ladder. Bizarrely, this ethnic pecking-order could sometimes trump a man's formal rank. So that a Filipino captain, perhaps physically small as most of his countrymen were, could seem a far less authoritative figure than his tall, beefy Ukrainian second-in-command. And it was depressing to sometimes see a Filipino officer choose to eat with the crew rather than alongside his fellow officers. Despite the definite sense of 'family' that you'd usually find among a ship's crew, it was also true that the less appealing aspects of the human race didn't always disappear when afloat.

At the risk of sounding like a pompous git, Mum and Dad had brought me up to treat everyone the same, no matter how lowly their station in life. So you should talk to a dustman the same way you'd talk to a duke, even though the latter were thin on the ground in Blackpool. I called everyone 'sir', including the cooks and the most ordinary seamen, at least till I got to know their names; though one captain raised a snooty eyebrow and told me it wasn't 'appropriate'.

On every voyage, I felt it mattered that the security team not only behaved like professionals, but dressed that way too. It was one strategy for gaining the confidence of the captain and crew, especially on those jobs where they'd been reluctant to have us aboard.

'Jeez, what do you look like?' I sometimes had to say to new recruits on the first day of a transit.

'What's the problem Jordan?'

'You're at work here mate,' I'd reply. 'You're not on the beach at bloody Benidorm. Go and change please.'

In the merchant navy, the captain and the officers nearly always wore a uniform of white shirt with stripes and epaulettes denoting their rank. I didn't want my teams to look like a bunch of scruffs in comparison. So it was always clean polo shirts and smart cargo pants with the logo of the security company. Deck shoes, but no flip-flops.

'Aw c'mon, Jord!'

'No fucking flip-flops,' I'd hiss back.

The common factor among the 'flip-flop brigade' was in hoping to leave behind them some of the more irritating aspects of the military ethos. They'd had their fill of polishing buttons and boots and didn't like the concept of any sort of 'uniform' at all. Often, these were the guys who, as I've said, regarded their new careers as a bit of a holiday in the sun. However disciplined and effective they might be in the event of any pirate attack, they'd come onto the ship with the wrong attitude. They just hadn't grasped that they were guests in somebody else's place. It was usually due to such blokes that any tensions would come to the surface.

Usually these boiled down to simple issues of respect, especially with regard to the captain. Some of the flip-flop brigade, who'd maybe served under the most distinguished commanders in the British Army, weren't always that impressed by some guy who, in their eyes, was merely shifting a load of frozen prawns or 100,000 T-shirts destined for the shelves of Primark. So they didn't think twice about plonking their arses in the captain's chair on the bridge or putting their feet up on his chart table. They might try on his cap for a laugh or use his personal binoculars, altering the focus which had been set for his eyesight.

To some of the crew, this was almost tantamount to blasphemy. One story I heard was about a ship off Mombasa. An outraged officer secretly filmed the security team leader lolling in the captain's chair, playing on a laptop and neglecting his duties. The culprit finally realised what was going on, fists flew and the officer was knocked out cold. But that wasn't the end of the drama, just the beginning. Contracts to provide security to the larger shipping chains could be worth massive amounts of money to the Private Maritime Security Companies. In the Mombasa case, the PMSC lost a deal worth 14 million euros and began to go downhill soon after. A similar fuck-up occurred in the Seychelles when a PMSC team leader smuggled 200,000 cigarettes aboard in order to sell them back in the UK. The local customs people got a tip-off and boarded the ship, causing costly delays and imposing a heavy fine on the shipping company. The team leader was sacked and the PMSC had to do the job for free in order to retain the client. In both these cases, all the trouble was caused by two guys with a shitty attitude.

You needed to show respect not just towards individuals

but towards cultures too. For instance, the casual effing and blinding of your average British ex-squaddie could easily create an aggressive impression and intimidate gentler, more polite peoples like the Filipinos. Too often, I'd need to take one of the team aside for a quiet word.

'Hey Tommy, do me a favour and tone down the language.'

'You what?'

'Some of the crew find it offensive. It's not acceptable where they come from. You're not in the barracks any more, mate.'

'Aw c'mon, Jord.'

That same old moan again. Sometimes I felt I was playing nanny to some of these guys, but this stuff mattered. Nor was it a great idea to sneak into the galley in the middle of the night to make toast and leave a right old mess for the chef to clear up in the morning. There were a hundred little ways you could piss people off. To do your job successfully, you need to avoid as many of them as you could. At the end of every transit, the captain would write a report for his shipping company on the security team's performance. Even without really serious incidents like the flying fists in Mombasa, a few minor storms in a tea-cup during a voyage could very well lead to your company, and of course yourself, never being hired again.

For security teams invited onto merchant ships, it was one thing to be a cuckoo in the nest; to be a bull in a china shop was something else entirely. In the military, if you screwed up on duty or misbehaved off duty, you'd get your wrists well slapped and, unless it was a really serious issue, that would be that. No further consequences. But in commerce, no excuses would ever be accepted for bad performance. Cock-ups usually cost money. It was a different ball-game entirely.

On the whole though, with a bit of give and take, security teams rubbed along pretty well with the crews we lived and worked with. Real friendships, however temporary, were often formed and it was always a pleasure to go on a transit and bump into a friendly face I'd known on some other ship. I got a lot out of mixing with guys from other countries and cultures. It was fascinating to pick up the different characteristics of the various races; Indians, Greeks, Russians, Filipinos, Italians, Yemenis, Omanis. There was almost always something new and valuable to learn from their stories. I was determined to get as much as possible out of this new life of mine; not just the money rolling into the bank.

I always told my teams never to reveal to the ships' crews how much they were earning. The seafarers had a pretty good idea we were coining it and often tried to worm it out of us, but it wouldn't have been a good idea at all. As a security team, we needed their cooperation and their goodwill, not their envy and bitterness. So it wasn't a good idea to tell them that we often earned in a day what they were paid in a month.

Not all the ships were luxurious. There were many times I thought longingly of the five-star conditions on my first transit, the spanking new *Suez Cape Ann* with the Jacuzzi, the gym and the cinema. Your heart would sink when you got to the dock, or were ferried out to the mooring, only to discover you were about to spend two or three weeks on an old rust-bucket or even occasionally, on an out-and-out shit-heap that should have been scuttled long ago. Thankfully, the rates of pay tended to be pretty much the same whether the ship was decent or not, but that didn't always compensate for the conditions.

The older Chinese vessels could be especially grim. Cockroaches were often members of the crew. One day I woke up with an itchy rash on my wrist and between my fingers, so I went to the medical officer.

'What's this then doc?'

'It's scabies,' he said wearily. He'd obviously seen it all before.

'Fucking hell. You've got to be joking,' I replied, forgetting my own rules about bad language.

But he wasn't. We soon worked out that I'd caught it from a blanket that hadn't been laundered because the clapped-out washing machines had broken down yet again. It was a nasty experience. The itching was bloody awful. I had to be covered in a lotion from neck to toe, as did anyone else I'd been physically close to or whose hand I might have shaken. I'd always thought scabies was a sexually transmitted infection, so I was hacked off to get it without even the compensatory shag.

I could only hope the doc knew what he was doing. Every vessel had to have a so-called medic on board; there were always accidents of one sort or another, like people losing thumbs in machinery. In a real emergency, the captain would radio for a helicopter to airlift the sick or injured to the nearest hospital, but for anything less serious you relied on these guys. You never asked to see their qualifications, but it was unlikely any of them would ever end up in Harley Street. I always prayed I'd never need one of them to stitch a bollock back on.

After the scabies, I took my own sleeping-bag on every job. It often seemed wiser to place it on the floor rather than on some dodgy-looking mattress. Sometimes I'd be unlucky enough to have to share a cabin, either with one of my own team or with a crew member who maybe didn't speak much English or have high-end personal habits. Your precious sleep was disturbed when they got up to go about their duties or on their shift, keeping watch for a pirate attack. After a few restless nights and scorching hot days, even the most easy-going tempers could fray at the edges. All you could do was count down the days till you'd reach port.

It wasn't always the close proximity of others that caused tensions. It could often be the food. On an Indian ship, it might be curry three times a day. On a Chinese vessel, you could find yourself eating chickens' feet and rice for a whole fucking fortnight. Another Chinese speciality was fish-heads; just the heads mind you, the rest of the fish having been thrown away, which made no sense at all to us. One night, a sumptuous dish of bright green ice-cream was presented to us with a great flourish. Sick to the stomach of fish-heads, we fell on it like ravenous beasts, assuming it was mint-flavoured. It wasn't. It was onion ice-cream and we nearly threw it back up. It was amazing how quickly this could transform a bunch of cheery British lads into early-stage depressives or even psychopaths. Sometimes, you'd have killed your granny for a bacon sandwich.

Take the Case of The Egg On Toast. Rocky Mason, now dried out after his dive from the *Biscaglia*, was one of my regular team-mates. After two weeks of fish-heads and rice, he was half-mad with hunger for a decent meal. Unable to stand it any longer, he'd used all his survival skills to track down two solitary eggs in the chef's stores. Convinced that these were probably the last two eggs this side of the Suez Canal, he'd stashed them away somewhere safe, planning to eat them after his watch. But he hadn't hidden them well enough. His colleague Chris Docherty, also searching every nook and cranny, had stumbled across the eggs. When Rocky came off his watch, he entered the galley to find Chris wolfing down egg on toast. All hell broke loose, all team discipline went out of the porthole.

'Where did you get those eggs?'

'Found them at the back of a cupboard,' replied Chris, munching away.

'Those are *my* fucking eggs.'

'What do you mean Rocky?'

'I'm the one who found them first. I was saving them for later.'

'Oh, sorry mate, but how was I to know that?' said Chris. 'Do you want a bite?'

'A bite? I'll bite your bloody head off. Those were my eggs, you bastard.'

And it escalated from there. Two furious men, both trained in mortal combat, screaming at one another over a plate of eggs on toast. I came scurrying to see what the drama was and managed to calm it down. If I hadn't, one or the other of them might have ended up being thrown overboard. It was funny of course, but it showed how quickly people could get agitated in a hot-house situation.

Nor was it ideal that the captain and some of the crew witnessed the worst of it. It wasn't till we eventually disembarked in Egypt and I bought each of them a Cadbury's Creme Egg that they recovered their sense of humour and were firm friends again.

These daft dramas were all part of the learning-curve of living on the ships. Eventually most of us would bring our favourite treats to see us through, as well as vitamins and nutrients to balance our diet. Being totally fit was a major part of the job and it was hard to feel you were in peak condition if your shit was 90 per cent rice.

But there was plenty of fun, too. As part of the bonding process, the security team would always be expected to perform at the crew's weekly karaoke night. For Filipinos in particular, for reasons I never grasped, karaoke was like a religion. The star of these gigs was often Dave McFarland, known to all as 'Macca'. He came from Carrickfergus in Northern Ireland and had an Irish accent thick as a peat-bog, which had taken me a good while to be able to understand. Macca was about 40 by then; a real old sea-dog, ex-Royal Navy and a former bouncer. He was a soccer fanatic and when off-duty, never wore anything other than a Northern Ireland football shirt. Macca had a wonderful outgoing personality and the merchant crews always loved him. The sight of this big burly Irishman belting out *Sweet Caroline* never failed to reduce a bunch of Filipino seafarers to a mixture of hysterical laughter and fervent admiration. It was a performance that Neil Diamond himself might have applauded. The truly bizarre thing was that, because of the strict no-alcohol rule, it had to be done stone-cold sober. Not easy. Trust me; just try it some time.

There were good times ashore, too. Not every voyage was a straight A to B job through Pirate Alley. Sometimes the ship would be on a circuit of multiple ports around the Indian Ocean, from Aden in the west to Sri Lanka in the east. Although many commercial ports, such as the vast Balhaf in Yemen, were unappealing places with no compensating social life in an adjacent town, others were oases of pleasure after the desert of the sea.

Since the days of the Phoenicians, Romans and ancient Greeks, the presence of large numbers of seafarers with money in their pockets and a twitch in their pants had had a big impact on the local communities where they ended up. The influx of ex-military men onto merchant shipping was also a Gold Rush for plenty of other happy people: the airlines flying these guys to their embarkation ports; the posh hotels in which, like spoiled brats, we now expected to be billeted; the companies who offered scuba-diving, water-skiing and excursions to help us kill time while we waited for our ship to come in; the local agents who dealt with the admin on behalf of the ship owners, usually in some far distant country. And above all, the owners of restaurants, clubs, bars, bazaars and brothels in the harbours around the Indian Ocean. We were seen as fat cats and the parasites descended, rubbing their hands with glee. It was Christmas all year round.

Of course, boys will be boys and things could sometimes get boisterous, though it was usually harmless enough. If the locals got a bit cheesed off with late-night revelry and a few pools of sick on the prom, they mostly closed their eyes and thought of their profit margins.

As time went on and regulations got tighter, most security companies imposed strict no-booze rules on their teams during the voyage itself. British guys usually took this on the chin but it once led me into deep water when I tried to impose teetotalism on a crew which was mostly French. Drinking wine with their meals was as natural to them as breathing, so I found myself facing a second French Revolution, though I eventually got my way. Even in a brief stopover, my teams rarely had more than one glass of wine with dinner; we were responsible for the security of the vessel whether it was in the middle of the ocean or tied up at a jetty. I was always glad I never had any dramas with drugs on board. Unlike on the *Maersk Alabama* where, long after the famous attack, two American security guards died of a drug overdose while the ship was actually in Pirate Alley.

But the more usual trouble was in the waiting periods between transits, when draconian rules couldn't really be imposed. However abstemious British lads might be on the job, getting hammered as soon as they were off-duty is as much of a military tradition as Trooping The Colour. Shameful maybe but, like it or not, it's just in the culture. Maybe it's something to do with the crushing discipline under which soldiers spend most of their days; when the leash is finally off, they go a bit wild. That's certainly happened in some of those 'flesh-pots' around the Indian Ocean. In the beautiful, historic town of Galle in Sri Lanka, the glorious beach became almost like a rest and recuperation camp. Likewise, a bar called The Lucky Tuna where British guys often upset the locals, pestered the women and got into the odd fight. In a luxury hotel on

Mauritius, drunken security guys ruined the honeymoon of a British couple, who'd probably saved up for it for years, by pissing in the swimming pool and being generally objectionable. Bad stuff. The trouble was that grubby behaviour could stick like mud to the reputation of the company you worked for. In time, its business might decline and you'd find yourself out of work. As you knocked back that one beer too many, you might well be cutting your own throat. After a while, many locals stopped being so glad to see the Gold Rush guys. Not just because of the trouble they could bring, but because ordinary tourists began to avoid these places.

Sometimes however, the security teams weren't the perpetrators, but the victims. Pockets stuffed with money, they could be easy prey. On Reunion Island, in 2011, an ex-Marine called Carl Davies was found murdered. He'd been out on the town with his team-mates and the captain of his ship, but had left alone to walk back to the vessel. The next morning his body was found; having been beaten, stabbed and thrown off a cliff into a ravine. It was also claimed that he'd been sexually assaulted before his death. But his cash and valuables were untouched. The authorities were accused of trying to cover it up in order to protect tourism, but Carl's family went on campaigning for justice and wouldn't give up. Only in June 2017 was one of the suspects found guilty of murder and jailed for 15 years. Four others have yet to be tried, so the fight goes on.

The case of Carl Davies was a wake-up call to me and to everyone. What happened to him could have happened to any of us. It was a sharp reminder that guys like us were far from home and not always as welcome as we fondly imagined. Security guards had to look after our own security too and be very watchful; there was safety in numbers. Sometimes, there could be a 'gung-ho' attitude, a cocky carelessness that could have serious consequences; more than a few guys died from malaria because they hadn't been bothered to have the proper vaccinations before leaving home. Occasionally, that 'hard man' vibe could expose just how vulnerable we all really are.

I'd soon realised that, in my new industry, it was vital to maintain the military discipline that most of us had been taught and not to drift away from it in any way. On many ships, the captain would host a barbecue on deck at the end of a voyage or perhaps when crossing the Equator. If it had been a safe transit, he might want to thank the security team, relax the rules and have a farewell beer with them. You didn't want to offend the captain who you may have grown to like, but the no-booze-aboard rule really mattered. It was always tricky, always a finely balanced judgment. Even more awkward, the captain might ask for a photo taken with him holding your gun, if you had one. But it was an unbreakable rule that team weapons were never ever passed to crew members, even when unloaded.

'Oh come on, Jord,' he might say 'My grandkids would love it. Old Grandad with a gun. Nobody's going to know.'

But what if somebody did? What if somehow, for some malicious reason maybe, that photo found its way online or into a newspaper? It would pander to all the worst misconceptions of what armed security guards were doing. That old 'mercenary' smell again. I certainly didn't want a pic of myself splashed across a tabloid, with a rifle in one hand and a beer in the other. That just wasn't what I was here for. I was a professional; my job to protect the lives and livelihoods of these guys. Not to be grinning out from a photo frame in their little flat in Manila. After my first year or so on the ships, I was ever more aware of the faults of this game and ideas were beginning to take shape in my mind about what I might do to change things for the better.

As Dad had reminded me, I had once been in the King's Royal Hussars.

'In some ways you always will be. Live up to that.'

CHAPTER 8

Preparing for the Worst

As we headed into the port, the helicopter appeared out of the sky and circled above the ship. A voice barked down to us by radio.

'Drop your weapons now!'

The captain and I looked at each other. What on earth were they on about?

'We have no weapons,' the captain replied into the radio. 'This ship is unarmed.'

'I repeat,' said the voice, even more emphatically,' drop your weapons now or we will be forced to take action.'

'This ship carries no weapons,' replied the captain again. 'You are mistaken. I repeat, we are unarmed.'

The helicopter was hovering even lower now, its rotor blades sending violent ripples across the dead-calm water.

It had been an uneventful transit, boring even. Not a pirate to be seen. Not so much as what we called a 'suspicious approach', let alone anything resembling a real threat. After two weeks at sea, we were looking forward to the feel of dry land under our feet and a decent dinner. Trouble was, this wasn't just any old port, this was Balhaf, that vast, multimillion-dollar gas terminal in Yemen. The port where I'd boarded my very first ship, the *Suez Cape Ann*. The port that was a constant terrorist target and where security was merciless. We had just radioed to ask for a naval escort into this ultra-sensitive harbour. Instead, the helicopter had appeared. What the hell was their problem?

The voice now shouted across the radio.

'There is an armed man positioned at the stern of your ship. He must lay down his weapon at once or we will take immediate military action!'

The captain and I looked at each other, with a combination of total confusion and rising alarm. Then the penny dropped. The helicopter was right. There *was* a man on guard at the stern. It was Dick. And it was me who'd posted him there.

Dick had been stationed on the stern 24 hours a day, seven days a week for the past two weeks. From a distance, he must have looked quite scary, which was of course the point. Dressed in camouflage colours and a tin helmet, he gave the impression of being a lean, mean fighting-machine. A real action hero. If you messed with Dick, you'd regret it. He was an incredible guy. He needed no sleep, no food, no drink. And despite his tough appearance, he was a great bloke who never upset anyone with a hard word or bad behaviour. Everybody loved him. Yes, you've guessed it. Dick was a dummy.

In fact, there was more than one Dick. While he guarded the stern, his twin brothers, Dicks 2,3 and 4, had been positioned on the bridge wings and various other key spots around the ship. On transits where the security team was unarmed, these dummies were often used to give the impression to approaching pirates that the ship was bristling with weapons and that they'd do well to bugger off sharpish. On this occasion, I'd remembered to remove Dick's brothers as we'd got close to Balhaf, but I'd completely forgotten Dick himself. Shit.

The only downside of using the dummies was the possibility that instead of deterring pirates, they could escalate a tense situation. It wasn't always a great idea to make people believe you had weapons when actually you didn't. And that was just what was happening here. We now had a Yemeni helicopter buzzing above us, with its crew on red alert and its guns pointed straight at us. Unlike Dick's gun, these were very much for real. Bloody hell.

My face flushed bright-red on top of my already sun-tanned face. Who was the dummy now?

'The figure on the stern is a dummy! It's not real,' I shouted into the radio.' We will remove it at once.'

But the helicopter was still suspicious. It wanted proof. To satisfy them, Dick had to be thrown overboard.

I dashed out to the stern, picked up Dick and waved him around towards the helicopter, trying to convince them that he was no more substantial than a Guy Fawkes on bonfire night. Then, with a dramatic gesture, I hurled Dick over the side and watched him float away in the foamy wake of the ship. Sorry Dick. We'll miss you.

Luckily for me, everyone saw the funny side; the helicopter, the captain and the crew. The cock-up wasn't reported back to my bosses. But the death of Dick was a lesson well-learnt. In tense circumstances, even a small human error might just have serious consequences. Attention to detail was vital. There could be no excuses. Not the heat of the sun, not boredom, not a bad night's sleep. Nothing.

Amid all the laughter, it's no exaggeration to say that the

drowning of Dick was a slight sadness for the crew. They'd made him with their own hands; he was their very own Frankenstein's monster. I often held competitions among the crew to see who could build the most realistic dummy. Usually, the results were pretty scrappy but, in the case of Dick, a lot of work had gone into him. The ship's highly skilled welders and fabricators had got involved and Dick had been far more than just a man of straw. He was a Rambo, a prince among dummies. To see him drift away out into the Gulf of Aden almost brought a tear to the eye.

But the need to make daft dummies shows how often we had to resort to *'Blue Peter'* methods to improve the security of a ship. I always tried to find out something about a vessel before I even reached the dockside, so that I had some rough idea of its strengths and weaknesses. A thorough risk assessment was always the foundation of any security plan. But sometimes the impression you got online was far removed from the reality of what greeted you when you reached the top of the gangway. There were plenty of times when Dave 'Macca' McFarland or Rocky Mason and I huddled together after a swift recce.

'So what d'you think Rocky?' I'd say in a low voice so the captain couldn't hear.

'Sitting duck.'

'Macca?'

'Fuckin' hell Jord. Let's go home.'

'Too late mate.'

The trouble was that if the BMP4 'bible' of basic protection measures wasn't already there, you probably had no time to implement it. If you needed enough razor-wire to protect a bloody great container vessel, you couldn't just buy it from the nearest chandler's. And shipping companies liked a fast turnaround; they had deadlines for cargo delivery and penalties if they failed to meet them. It was in those situations, you found yourself improvising. The creation of the dummy guards was just one of the weirder ones.

However bizarre it was, it at least had the advantage of engaging the crews in the business of their own safety. Because, apart from physical protection of the ship itself, your best bet against the pirates was the efficient training of the seafarers themselves. It was this, or the lack of it, that would make the crucial difference between a ship being successfully hijacked and a ship that got away.

The training process required a balancing act. It was vital that the crew took it very seriously and applied themselves to learning the techniques. At the same time, we needed to do it in a calm, professional manner. There was nothing to be gained from scaring the shit out of them. The presence of a security team on board certainly provided reassurance but was also a tangible reminder of the really bad stuff now happening in the seas they'd criss-crossed so often in perfect safety.

Whatever cheerful front the crew might put on, there were plenty who were indeed scared to some degree. In some ways, the merchant navy was a small world and modern communications made sure that news of every pirate attack, successful hijack and hostage-taking was soon known by nearly every seafarer in the merchant navy. Naturally ship owners and seafarers alike, clung to the comfort-blanket that still only a small minority of ships were targeted. But by 2011, the year in which pirate attacks reached their all-time high, nobody was in any doubt as to what their fate might possibly be if their vessel was the unlucky one. The tales, often grim, of what had happened to hostages, spread fast.

As the months went by and the crisis deepened, seafarers lifted their heads out of the sand and grudgingly came to appreciate the need for security teams on their ships and that it might be well worth squashing up a bit to accommodate these cuckoos in their floating nest. Far better that the chef should undercook everyone's fish-heads and rice once or twice than that he should skip a training session and run around in an emergency like one of his own headless chickens. Far better that Muslim crew members should delay one of their five daily prayer-periods for half an hour to learn how to safeguard their lives.

The simple, prime objective in training the seafarers was that they should know what to do in the event of a suspicious approach, an illegal boarding or an actual hijack. Nobody expected them to grab a gun and fight back; that was our job. The essence of their responsibility was to make themselves safe. The first level of alert to be broadcast was called *Code Yellow*. Three rings on the ship's bell or three toots on the horn, followed by a Tannoy announcement. *Code Yellow* meant that potential pirates had been sighted and/or a suspicious approach was under way. The crew must drop whatever they were doing and muster at a prearranged spot below decks. Each man had already been given a personal number. At the mustering point, a roll-call was taken; each person had to shout out his number, so that everyone was instantly accounted for and there was no need to search every cabin, shower or TV room. Just one person missing and the whole concept of group safety would be wrecked. At the mustering point, the crew would wait for information coming down from the bridge on how the drama was developing.

If the situation got worse, the threat was upgraded to Code Red. This told everyone that a definite attack was now under way and that the ship was in imminent danger. Their priority was to get the hell out of harm's way so that nobody could be seized by the attackers and instantly transformed from an ordinary sailor into a hostage with a high price on his head.

So let's suppose that you're me, a private security guard on a ship heading into Pirate Alley. You're feeling pretty confident that everything possible has been done to protect it in the event of an attack. You've done a detailed risk assessment and worked out your security plan for this particular ship. The razor-wire is all round the decks, sharp as dragon's teeth. The high-pressure hoses are primed and ready to pump out hundreds of litres of water; enough to blow a gang of sumo-wrestlers off their feet. You've drilled the crew so vigorously that they hear your voice in their sleep. You've won the acceptance and respect of the captain and the officers. If trouble comes, they will turn to you and your team as their protectors.

And then it happens. Trouble does come. It will often start as nothing more than a tiny white speck on a radar screen, like a bit of dandruff on a dark jacket. The duty officer on the bridge shouts out to where I'm stationed on the bridge-wing, scanning the sea.

'Mr Wylie sir, come and look at this, please.'

Sure enough, two small dots will be advancing on us from the perimeter of the radar screen. Trouble is, they could be anything. Radars are imperfect. They only tell you that something is out there, not what it is. The purpose of the radar on commercial ships isn't scanning for pirates, it's for safety; picking up the presence of other large vessels nearby in order to avoid collision, especially at night. Most nautical radar is cluttered by 'ghosts'; presences visible on the screen that could be any one of a dozen things. Often your 'pirate' might just be the caps of the waves. But ships' radars offer different degrees of capability. Ironically, the higher-frequency equipment on the larger vessels is less useful in the context of security; designed to filter out waves and other small objects... like pirate skiffs. Not exactly helpful then.

When I first started out as a security guard, I assumed the tiniest speck on the screen was suspicious, which often amused the duty officer with his more experienced eye. I soon learned to reserve my judgment in case it was no more than a breadcrumb from his lunch. But sometimes, even the experienced seafarer, like a doctor with a scan, could only make a tentative diagnosis.

'So what do you reckon?' I'd ask. 'You're the expert.'

'At the moment, I can't be sure. But we need to keep a close watch.'

I always told my security teams that there was no technology more reliable than the Mark 1 Human Eyeball. If the radar threw up something worrying, we'd be right out on the bridge-wing searching the seas with our binoculars or our night-vision goggles. If there was enough manpower available, we'd rope in the crew to stand watch at different positions around the ship. Pulse rates went up. What the fuck was out there? Was it nothing more than a few stroppy waves or the start of a life-changing incident? This uncertainty, this bloody great question-mark, would always be the central feature of my life on the ships. What would I have to do in the next few minutes or hours?

The good news was that by now the International Maritime Organisation (IMO) had laid down a clear series of procedures for shipping in the event of any sort of 'suspicious approach'. Naturally, these all boiled down to getting help as fast as possible.

Once our eyes had confirmed that the radar 'dandruff' represented approaching skiffs, the captain's first step was to activate the Ship Security Alert System, usually by pressing a button concealed somewhere on the bridge. This tells the security manager at the headquarters of the shipping company that the vessel was under threat. This manager then contacts the ship to confirm that it isn't a false alarm. If an attack is confirmed, this triggers a whole series of events. In the swanky offices, the ship owners, their insurers, kidnap and ransom specialists and hostage negotiators all gather. Like greyhounds straining in the slips, they're ready to go. But first they have to sit and wait and see how bad this is going to get.

Back on the ship, the captain's next action is to use his satellite-phone to contact United Kingdom Maritime Trade Operations (UKMTO), based in Dubai. This discreetly titled body is, in effect, the nautical equivalent of dialling 999. Set up in the aftermath of the Twin Towers attack to monitor the general maritime security situation in the troubled Middle East, from 2007 its role had become largely focused on the fight against piracy. At UKMTO, the progress of every ship passing through the Indian

Ocean, the Arabian Sea and the Gulf of Aden was monitored 24/7. After brushing his teeth and eating his cornflakes, the first thing any sensible captain does every single morning is to inform UKMTO of the ship's exact position. In the event of a suspicious approach or a definite attack, it is UKMTO who sends out the cavalry; alerting the international naval forces to get to you fast with their ships and helicopters. The trouble is, of course, the sheer size of the area and the limited resources of those navies; that old comparison of patrolling the whole of Europe with eight police cars.

Unfortunately, it isn't always possible to know if your SOS has got through; the ship might be in a signal 'blackspot' and you might be talking to the endless, empty sea. If you don't get a response, it's wise to fear the worst. Another problem is that it might not be just the cavalry who heard the SOS. The pirates might hear you too because everyone can easily access Channel 16, the default radio frequency used in these situations, More than a few times, I'd go on air and pretend to be an officer belonging to the naval forces, assuring the captain of the threatened ship that help was on its way.

But even if the cavalry is indeed rushing towards you, you and your ship are, for the time being at least, still out there on your own. And possibly in very deep shit. Which is exactly why the job of guys like me is to make sure that your lonely monster of iron and steel is as impregnable as possible, till help finally arrives. The obvious analogy is with those great medieval castles. The Tower of London is a good example; so are the massive Welsh fortresses built by Edward I such as Harlech and Carnarvon. These were all conceived around the concept of 'layered defence'. An outer ring of walls, then one or more inner rings. If the outer ring was breached, the defenders of the fortress would retreat behind the next layer and so on. If these secondary layers didn't hold either, they would eventually flee inside the strongest bastion of all. The last resort. The castle keep.

In the first decade of the 21st century, off the Horn of Africa, the world's merchant fleets adopted the exact same principle. Instead of battlements and boiling oil, our outer layers of defence were the razor-wire, the high-pressure hoses, the sonic deterrents, even Dick the Dummy and his brothers. If those failed, the next layer was the firmly defended entry-points to the bridge and the rest of the superstructure, especially the engine room; locked and reinforced doors at every level, stairways sealed off by strong grilles.

Another layer is the human one. You just hoped and prayed that, if the worst happened, the training you'd given the captain, the officers and the crew meant that they'd stay cool and perform the roles you'd given them, both to prevent a successful hijack and to safeguard their own lives. But sometimes things don't quite go as you'd hope. If panic and confusion come in through the door, discipline could go out through the porthole. We're all flesh and blood after all.

So if, for whatever reason, the game was lost, the defenders have to retreat as quickly and as calmly as possible to the 'keep'. On today's merchant ships, this is simply a 'safe-room', buried in the bowels of the hull, where the crew is protected from harm till the cavalry arrives. Usually it is called by another name. The Citadel.

'This is the *ensuite* then?' asked the first officer, contemplating the objects in the corner of the room. Three yellow plastic window-cleaner's buckets.

'Yep,' I replied. 'Afraid so.'

'Well,' he said, 'let's just pray for a mass outbreak of constipation.'

If the worst came to the worst, this was how 20 or so men would have to perform their basic functions, perhaps for several days. There was no surrounding cubicle or partition, not even a carefully positioned potted plant. All privacy would be lost, all dignity gone. The prospect was far from appealing.

It was no good pretending to the crew that our time in the Citadel, if it came, would be a sweet-smelling bed of roses. In no way would it ever be looked back on as a happy memory. But it was important to familiarise them with the space, teach them in advance where everything was kept and to reduce, as much as possible, the fear they might have at the idea of being locked inside it for a long period. Sure, it might be physically unpleasant and emotionally stressful, but it would, unless something went badly wrong, be safe.

The concept of the 'safe-room' is hardly new. It had been a security staple on land for many years. Sensitive government and military installations often had them, as did the homes of the seriously rich, but they'd almost never existed aboard merchant ships. So when Somali piracy suddenly created the urgent need for their use at sea, it usually had to be an improvised, makeshift arrangement, the conversion of an existing space. On the 'castle keep' principle, this space needed to be already protected behind several outer layers of defence. In a ship, this meant as deep down in her guts as possible. Often, the best bet was a smaller room off the engine room; the engine control room or the steering-gear room. In an ideal world, the means of propelling the ship and its other vital systems would be inside that space so the attackers couldn't gain access to them.

There is no doubt that the principle of the 'safe-room' worked. As the geographical area of attacks were spreading further out into the Indian Ocean and the likely response-times of the warships and helicopters became longer, the Citadel proved its worth again and again.

By the height of the piracy phenomenon, there were dozens of incidents where the pirates had successfully boarded a ship but had abandoned an attempted hijack because everyone with the ability to control the vessel was well out of their reach. After the crew's physical safety, this was of course the second stonking great reason for removing the entire crew from the clutches of the intruders. Without the crew to control it, the pirates were riding on the back of a giant creature not one of them knew how to tame.

It was a seriously good idea to stop the bastards finding the Citadel in the first place. The interiors of these ships were often vast; behind the open expanse of the main engine room were warrens of smaller spaces and if your system of outer defences held firm, it was entirely possible that the attackers might never locate the Citadel, especially if it had somehow been possible to camouflage its entry. The attackers knew perfectly well that the crew would have sent out distress signals and that help was possibly on its way, but they had no idea how much time they had before it arrived. Was it worth spending several hours burrowing around below decks trying to find the Citadel, especially if the captain had 'blacked out' the lighting systems? Often, if the attack was opportunistic and not well planned, they'd decide that it wasn't and just flee with whatever swag they could easily lay hands on; laptops, iPads and other personal possessions.

But if the ship was a spectacular prize, perhaps worthy of a multimillion-dollar ransom and the assault had been well plotted, they weren't going to abort it without a struggle. As the use of Citadels became more widespread, the pirates got correspondingly determined to breach the layered defences and reach the crew. They might try blowing off padlocks and bolts on outer doors and stairways, either with plastic explosives, their own weapons or with tools lying around on board, such as fire-axes, disk-cutters and crowbars. They might even try smoking out the crew with small fires beside the ventilation ducts; though most ships are riddled with vents and ducts so they might have trouble finding the right ones. But that was a dangerous practice to say the least, especially if there were a few thousand tons of liquid gas right under your arse.

The Citadel had to be equipped in advance with every-thing necessary for survival for several days. In such a tense and unique situation, it was important to maintain people's spirits and the belief that this would all soon be over. Providing life's basic necessities was an important element of that. First of all, there must be enough palata-ble, long-life food and plenty of water; the amounts care-fully calculated on the number of crew and the likely length of time we'd be stuck in there. There must be enough thick blankets or sleeping bags to cushion against a few nights on a metal floor. You must stock up on medical supplies to treat any illness or injury which might have occurred in the rush to safety, including anyone unlucky enough to have taken a bullet. And in the likelihood that the ship would be 'blacked-out', it would be dark in the Citadel, so battery-powered lamps and torches with plenty of spares had to be laid in.

Despite the smoke-out risk, the safe-room must have adequate ventilation even though, with 20 or 30 nervous, sweaty guys in there, it would still likely be as hot as hell. It also required portable fire extinguishing equipment in the event of a smoke-out or of some accident inside the room itself – though we'd have to disable any automatic fire suppression systems in case they activated and poisoned us all. Not much point in a place designed to help the crew stay alive, if it became their tomb instead.

Ideally the Citadel should have no more than one entry point. If there were any hatches, ventilation grilles or portholes, these needed to be locked and secured from the inside. So it was the 'front door' that was your drawbridge and portcullis rolled into one. You replaced any external hinges with internal ones. From the outside, it should look as little like an entrance as possible in the hope that it might just pass unnoticed.

On most commercial ships, these internal doors had never been designed to withstand any sort of aggressive assault. Certainly not a volley from an AK-47. Most conventional locks and hinges could be blown away like ducks on a rifle range. One of the most important jobs for the security team was to fortify all these internal doors to the max. You increased the basic strength of the door and its frame with long bolts of wood or steel, positioned both horizontally and vertically, which slid into plates welded onto the door frame and therefore couldn't be shot off. You also welded stoppers on each side of the door frame. All these doors were the 'layers' of your defence system. Their strength or weakness could be the major contributing factor in keeping everyone safe.

Above all, the Citadel needed to be able to talk to the outside world. This required a stand-alone communications system, independent of any other system on the ship, with a base-station within the Citadel itself. Its cabling had to be fed up onto the outer decks towards the antenna as discreetly as possible, in order to veil its existence from any sharp-eyed pirate who might decide to cut through it. For this stuff, it was always bloody useful to have an ex-Royal Signals guy on the security team. All the vital, up-to-date contact numbers were stored both on our satellite phones and as hard copies elsewhere in the room; the UKMTO in Dubai, the NATO Maritime Shipping Centre, the Maritime Security Centre for the Horn of Africa (MSCHOA) as well as the operations room of your own PMSC and the ship's owners in whichever country they were based. Basically, you had to reach out to anyone who might possibly help you when the shit hit the fan.

This capability of constant two-way communication between the occupants of the Citadel and potential rescuers was one of the prerequisites for any possibility of military or naval intervention. If the cavalry weren't pretty damn sure of the state of play on board a hijacked ship, there was no way they would gallop in. It was just too dangerous. That way you might end up with blood and brains on the decks, not necessarily belonging to the bad guys. The Charge of the Light Brigade wasn't a great idea.

Choosing the right moment to trigger *Code Red* and send the crew to the Citadel could be a tricky one. Too soon, and if the approach turned out to be a false alarm, you'd risk the development of future complacency and lack of urgency in a genuine crisis; 'the boy who cried wolf' scenario. Too late, and the pirates might well succeed in grabbing a hostage, either from the crew or the security team itself. In which case, the naval forces wouldn't intervene, it would be a successful hijack and the outrageous ransom demand would soon arrive at the shipping company's offices. Unless every single person reached safety in the Citadel, you, as a security team, would have completely and utterly fucked everything up. No pressure then.

But just as the deployment of security teams on merchant ships had initially met with resistance from both the ship owners and the international military forces, the use of Citadels wasn't universally approved of either. Lots of hand-wringing went on.

On the plus side, it was undeniable that the successful use of a safe-room won time for the cavalry to get there, perhaps even from a long distance. It stopped the pirates from being able to move the ship towards the nearest pirate land-base. Above all, it robbed them of their most important prize – the possession of potentially valuable hostages. All of that combined often made pirates throw up their hands in despair, decide life was too short and bugger off in search of easier prey.

On the negative side, the retreat to the Citadel meant that you'd effectively surrendered your ship to the attackers; you had in a sense 'failed'. And by herding the entire crew into one place, you'd done part of the pirates' job for them. They now knew that everyone was locked away, even if they didn't know where that was. They no longer needed to worry about any pocket of resistance; the sudden feel of an AK-47 being pushed into their back from some shady corner.

The voices raised against the use of Citadels also argued, quite rightly, that the emotional impact of being self-imprisoned could be extreme. The loss of privacy and personal dignity; the piss, the shit and the stink of sweaty bodies. The ignorance of what the intruders might be doing beyond the 'front door' and what they might be planning in order to reach the crew. The feeling of being rats in a trap, no longer in control of their own destiny. Just like soldiers in a battle situation, some seafarers were able to cope with that pretty well; others didn't. On the security team, we were always nervous of a panic breaking out. We'd look around the faces of the crew, wondering who might be the one to wobble or, heaven forbid, to crack. Panic could be a highly infectious thing.

Although statistics suggested that the Citadel template had worked in nearly nine out of 10 pirate attacks, that obviously left over 10 per cent of cases where it had been breached and overrun. Usually that was because of a badly chosen, vulnerable location, carelessness in strengthening the outer layers of defences or a loss of discipline in the retreat to the safe-room. Incredibly, pirates had sometimes even tricked a ship's crew into opening the 'front door'. So the Citadels would never be totally impregnable. In those medieval castles, the 'keep' did sometimes fall, for one reason or another.

But whatever their negatives, there was never any doubt in my own mind that Citadels had earned their stripes. Yet there was always a professional caveat to that. For me, the flight to the Citadel, however sensible, was a sort of defeat. A failure of our protective measures and of our training.

I always tried to live by the old military ethos of the '**7Ps**'. **P**rior **P**reparation and **P**lanning **P**revents **P**iss-**P**oor **P**erformance. If Jordan Wylie, Rocky Mason and Macca McFarland had done our stuff well, that Citadel should never need to be occupied. And those three yellow plastic buckets would stay empty.

CHAPTER 9

When Hostages Die

At regular intervals, I'd receive a sharp, salutary reminder of just why I was doing the job I did. Those ships which ventured into Pirate Alley without security, without a safe-room, sometimes paid a very heavy price for their complacency. Not just in terms of lost vessels or lost cargos, but in lost human lives.

Not every hijack was covered by the mass media, but the more spectacular ones usually were. Certainly, the attacks on small, private yachts would be all over the TV, press and internet. It was always easier for people to put themselves in the shoes of a middle-aged European couple on a pleasure craft than in those of 20 Filipino seafarers on a big ugly container ship. But whichever scenario hit the headlines, Somali piracy was usually good copy for the western media. It was often lurid, terrifying stuff.

My career at sea lasted from early 2010 till the middle of 2012. From shortly before my first transit and for six months after my last, 22 men were being held hostage on the *Iceberg-1*. In total, they were kept captive for about 1,000 days. So every single day I was on the ships, there existed concurrently a vivid example of the suffering which I was there to prevent.

She'd only been 10 miles out of Aden, loaded with

machinery, en route for the Emirates. The *Iceberg-1* was a roll-on, roll-off cargo vessel, a bit of a rust-bucket. The company who owned her had paid little attention to what was happening in the waters around the Horn of Africa. As usual, the pirate skiff had come roaring up out of nowhere, across a tranquil sea. The old ship had tried some evasive manoeuvres but she just wasn't fast enough. With their grappling hooks and ropes, they'd leeched onto her in no time. With their guns and rocket-propelled grenades, they'd soon taken control. And with the muzzle of an AK-47 at his head, the captain had been forced to turn the ship south towards Somalia.

At first, things had been bearable. Negotiations had started and the captain and crew had assumed their employers would pay up quickly. The ship and her cargo were well insured after all. But it soon became obvious that the ship's owners had little opinion of either the vessel or her crew. Ten million dollars? Dream on. The pirates must be joking. Weeks had stretched into months. The bargaining had gone on for a time, then gone quiet. Stalemate. Dead end. And that was when their hell really began, the full horror of which only came out after their release.

The crew was confined in the bowels of the ship, in a hold no more than 15 metres square. Twenty-two rats in a trap. The heat was unbearable, the conditions soon disgusting. They were given water that smelled of petrol. Their one daily meal was a bowl of dirty rice. Illness soon began. One man lost his eyesight.

As the weeks and months went by, the pirates got frustrated and jumpy. Moods made worse by whisky and by the *khat* leaves most Somali men chewed constantly to keep them alert; their teeth stained a sickly green by the juices. They squabbled and fought among themselves. Gradually, their impatience gave way to red-raw anger. Any hostage who protested about their conditions lived to regret it, though perhaps not for long. The first officer, pleading for treatment of the sick crewmen, had been beaten with electric cables with the others forced to watch.

It wasn't as if nobody knew they were there. The helicopters of the international forces often came to take a look at them and hovered for a while, but the rules of engagement decreed that they could never intervene and risk mass casualties. Instead of bringing hope, these aerial visits were soon dreaded by the hostages because they could trigger even worse treatment from the pirates.

As more time passed, the pirates lowered their expectations. There was still no sign of a ransom being paid; the ship owners seemed to have abandoned it. So how else might the pirates make a killing? Their answer to that question was literal. They would slaughter their captives and gut the bodies of their hearts and kidneys; there was always a good market for those. It was hardly the return they'd hoped for but better than nothing. The pirates teased the men with the prospect and gave them back their satellite phones so they could call their families to say farewell. It boggles the mind to imagine what these phone calls must have been like. But for some reason that remains unclear, the pirates' plans changed and these gruesome executions were never carried out.

Each day, the hostages were allowed a brief time to come up out of the stink of the hold and walk on the deck. Then a rifle-butt would prod them on the shoulder and they would troop back down away from the light. About five months into their ordeal, the third officer Wagdi Akram could stand it no longer. His mental health broke down and he took his own life by jumping into the sea.

On their eventual release, most of the crew faced not only post-traumatic stress disorder but a long, cruel struggle for compensation from the shipping company. The case of the *Iceberg-1* is one of the most notorious in the annals of the Somali piracy phenomenon but others were even more violent.

Unfortunately, it wasn't just the merchant shipping companies who were careless and complacent about sailing into the pirate-infested waters off the Horn of Africa. There were plenty of private individuals who were either unaware of, or just didn't pay enough heed to, what might be waiting for them on the high seas. These were the people who security guards like me simply couldn't protect.

The yacht was called *Tanit*, after the Phoenician goddess of the moon. On board were a young Frenchman from Brittany called Florent Lemacon, his wife Chloe and their three-year-old son Colin. It was going to be the journey of a lifetime. It was April 2009.

Florent was a computer programmer, bored with his conventional life. He and his wife felt it was high time to do something different, something bold. They would take some months out and point the prow of their 40-foot boat towards a wider, more exciting world. Having sailed safely through the Mediterranean and the Suez Canal, they picked up two family friends in Aden who would travel with them on the next leg of their journey towards Kenya and Zanzibar.

En route, the Lemacons had bumped into an older French couple named Delanne whose own yacht had been captured by six Somali pirates just six months earlier. The French president Nicolas Sarkozy had sent in marine commandos to rescue the Delannes. One pirate had been killed, the rest captured and taken to France to stand trial.

It was quite a story, especially as the Lemacons were about to enter the very waters where this drama had happened. But if it alarmed them, it didn't stop them. Perhaps they believed the old saying that lightning never struck twice in the same place. And anyway, the Delannes had lived to tell the tale. Nevertheless, on their blog of the voyage, they reported that they now sailed at night with their lights off.

But lightning did strike twice. The assault on the *Tanit* was almost a carbon copy of the previous one. Having seized the yacht, the pirates had turned towards the coast of Puntland in northern Somalia. But, as the hijack had begun, Florent Lemacon had managed to summon help and by now the tiny *Tanit* was being hotly pursued across the waves by five French and German frigates, working under the umbrella of the EU's *Operation Atalanta*. Although 70 commandos were on board and ready for action, the naval forces opened peaceful negotiations with the pirates, offering a ransom and even offering one of their own men in exchange for the release of Chloe Lemacon and little Colin. The pirates refused, holding out for a much bigger pot of money. But they were getting panicky by now and encircled by the military. On the radio channels, they were overheard debating the possibility of blowing up the yacht and executing the hostages.

That was it. The commandos zoomed in on the *Tanit* from every side. The pirates opened fire, the commandos fired back. All hell had broken loose, but the French forces somehow managed to get aboard the yacht. In its cramped confines, bullets were flying and Florent Lemacon was somehow killed in the crossfire. What exactly happened is unclear. Desperately trying to shield his wife and child from the mayhem, he may have lifted a mattress in front of them or merely raised his hand in front of his face. Whichever it was, in the heat of the moment, in a confusion of identities, this sudden movement may have been misinterpreted by one of the commandos. It was possible that Florent Lemacon had been killed in 'friendly fire' by the soldiers of his own country who were risking their own lives to save him and his family. It doesn't get much more tragic than that.

The operation to rescue the *Tanit* had freed four hostages including a young boy. The villains had been caught. Obviously though, it could hardly be called an unclouded success. Mixed in with the grief and sadness, there was a fair amount of criticism of the couple who, knowing the risks in the area, had nevertheless ploughed on. In their blog, the couple had recently posted, 'the danger is there... but the ocean is vast. The pirates must not be allowed to destroy our dream.'

Brave words, but now it seemed that the pirates had destroyed so much more than just a dream.

In the cabin of the Quest, four people lay dying in pools of blood. Two middle-aged American couples: Scott and Jean Adam from Los Angeles, the owners of the yacht, and their friends Bob Riggle and Phyllis Macay from Seattle.

Like the Lemacons, the four friends had set out on a voyage they'd hoped to remember for the rest of their lives. But in February 2011, 19 pirates aboard a mothership had tracked them down a couple of hundred miles off the coast of Oman. It was the first American vessel to be captured since the famous *Maersk Alabama* incident (the *Captain Phillips* ship) two years before.

As in the earlier case, the attackers' plan was to steer the Quest towards the coast of Somalia, in preparation to making a hefty ransom demand. But they reckoned without the US Navy, which instantly sent no less than an aircraft carrier, the *USS Enterprise*, plus three guided missile destroyers to the rescue. On finding the yacht, the naval forces started negotiations with the hijackers. But the pirates, no doubt shit-scared from being surrounded by this massive show of American power, were twitchy in the extreme. In the small hours of the morning, as talks were still going on, a pirate fired a rocket-propelled grenade towards one of the US vessels. It missed but, in a moment, what had been a fairly optimistic outcome for the hostages somehow went spectacularly wrong. Suddenly, the American forces heard gunfire aboard the little Quest. They didn't wait a second longer and launched a boarding-party to retake the yacht. In the ensuing shoot-out, two pirates were killed and the rest of them captured.

But Scott and Jean and Bob and Phyllis had been shot by their captors and, despite, immediate medical assistance, all four died inside the little cabin. As in the case of Florent Lemacon on the *Tanit*, it was a confused picture. The American forces claimed they'd been compelled to board the yacht once they'd heard the gunfire. But the unrepentant pirate kings in Somalia blamed the deaths on the naval assault, at the same time vowing revenge and moaning how much they'd invested in supplies, weaponry and wages for the attackers.

The captured pirates were taken to the USA, tried and sentenced to life in prison. It had always been a tricky process to actually convict the perpetrators of Somali piracy. There had been cases in the past when, after rescuing hostages, the naval forces had been pretty much compelled to let the pirates go, due to the complexities of international jurisdictions and even of an available prison in which to bang them up. But this time, the Americans were having none of that and were determined that the bastards paid their dues and that the awful deaths of Scott, Jean, Bob and Phyllis would be avenged.

From his hideaway, a pirate king called Farah had only one thing to say.

'Our business will go on,' he thundered.

Only six months after the death of Florent Lemacon, yet another feisty couple set sail on a similar voyage to get away from a conventional existence.

On a pitch-black, moonless night somewhere off the Seychelles, a skiff carrying eight armed pirates zoomed out of nowhere and attacked the *Lynn Rival*, a small yacht belonging to Paul and Rachel Chandler from Tunbridge Wells in Kent.

For just over a year, the Chandlers would be held in captivity on mainland Somalia. Living in various camps in the scorching Somali bush, they endured terrible conditions, being whipped, beaten, constantly threatened with execution and perhaps worst of all, being separated from one another. With a gun at their heads, they were forced, like so many hostages before and since, to make heartbreaking phone calls to their family for a ransom to be paid.

But the Chandlers' story featured one big difference from the hijacks of the other private yachts. Far from being worried about the chance of an armed rescue going tragically wrong, they were, after the event of course, absolutely incensed that nobody had attempted one. To this day, they remain angry about what they regard as a totally inadequate response from the British Government. A response, or rather the lack of it, which condemned them to 388 days of miserable, terrifying captivity before their ordeal ended.

Obviously these attacks on small craft were very different in scale to the hijacks suffered by huge container ships and oil tankers. But there were similarities too. The ransoms demanded were still extortionate. The human suffering was just as intense for those involved. They also underlined the glaring fact that by now it was bonkers for any vessel, large or small, commercial or private, to cross the Gulf of Aden or the Indian Ocean without armed security on board.

Of course that simply wasn't practical for small private boats, let alone desirable. Who the hell wanted to go on the romantic journey of a lifetime with a big hairy stranger like me riding shotgun? Not much fun for anyone. Nor would it be very likely that any individual yachtsman could himself repel a determined skiff of five or six pirates. So, for the time being at least, such intrepid folk would do well to stay in Brittany or Tunbridge Wells – or at least sail in a totally different direction from the Horn of Africa.

But a demand did soon arise for security guards on the super-yachts of the very wealthy. I signed on for a few such transits but it was a very strange experience after working on the big, sweaty ships of the merchant navy. The food was fabulous, the accommodation superb and it certainly smelt a lot better, but the vibe was utterly different. And though the people on board were nearly always nice, I felt that instead of being seen as a highly professional former soldier, I was often treated as something of an extra serv-ant, expected to fetch and carry, and it just wasn't for me.

It sometimes seemed surprising that the Somali pirates never targeted the large cruise liners that passed through Pirate Alley. In 1985, just four members of the Palestine Liberation Front had hijacked the Italian ship *Achille Lauro* off the coast of Egypt, holding the passengers hostage and killing one of them, an elderly, wheelchair-using Jewish-American named Leon Klinghoffer. This incident, though, was of just three days' duration and perhaps the Somali brigands felt that it would never be possible to either control or feed large numbers of people during the typical ransom process, which on average took around five months.

But the attacks on small private pleasure-craft still had an effect on everyone, including the merchant shipping industry. The stories of the Chandlers, the Lemacons and the two murdered American couples added to the mythol-ogy building up around Somali piracy. They added to the general nervousness now permeating those swanky ship-ping offices dotted around the capital cities of Europe and the USA, however well it might be concealed behind a corporate stiff upper lip. And also to the fears of seafarers when they packed their bags to go on their next trip across Pirate Alley and kissed their wives and children goodbye.

In the first years of Somali piracy, the received wisdom was that the brigands meant no harm to the people aboard the ships they targeted. Though a certain degree of aggression was undoubtedly involved, the earliest attacks were little more than 'smash and grab' raids in retaliation for the injustice of illegal fishing and toxic dumping. The main purpose being just to nick a few laptops, credit cards, some ready cash and scare the shit out of people so they'd think twice about invading Somali territory again. When all this had evolved into a serious business funded by organised criminals, its objective remained making money. So it was in the pirates' interest to protect the ship, its cargo and, above all, the people on board. The captives were, after all, the bargaining chips of the ransom demand. So why would you harm the geese who were going to lay your golden eggs and change your miserable life forever?

So that was the theory and, as a rule, it held good – as long as things were going well from the pirates' point of view. It was when things went pear-shaped that the danger would begin. When the ransom wasn't coming fast enough or even at all. When the rescue forces, for all the right reasons, were compelled to storm in. Or maybe just when patience snapped, when the misery of the captors became as great as that of the people they held prisoner. And then, all sense of common humanity was lost, terrible things were done and innocent men and women lay dead.

CHAPTER 10

Into Somalia

When Robin Hood was operating in Sherwood Forest, his business model was pretty straightforward. Taking from the rich, giving to the poor. There's nothing in the history books about him keeping a hefty chunk of it for himself and the lads in Lincoln green. Yet piracy in the waters off Somalia had started with the Robin Hood 'excuse' that it was a justifiable fightback against illegal fishing and the dumping of toxic waste. After all, said the pirates, the so-called government was too fucking useless to do it, so somebody else had to.

But, in an amazingly short period of time, the proceeds of piracy soared, reportedly peaking at a gobsmacking $230 million in 2010. As soon as the possibilities of making such vast sums dawned, the organised criminals moved in. It was inevitable of course. A bunch of grumpy, semi-literate fishermen with a cause could hardly deal with the complexities of negotiating with the sharp-brained operators of the international shipping companies.

In the way it began to operate, there was a striking parallel between Somali piracy and the drug trade. The big boys at the top who stayed in the shadows, provided the necessary funds, were the brains of the operations; then the lower echelons, the guys 'on the street'. No prizes for guessing who made the real fortunes. And so the 'pirate kings' of Somalia came into being. Sometimes they were just tribal chiefs who saw themselves as being pretty much above the law. But increasingly, they were criminals with highly organised networks. Though never proven, rumour even had it that money from their piracy ended up being laundered in London and New York. All of this was a long way from the skinny kid with a gun and a grievance.

One of the most famous 'pirate kings' was Mohamed Abdi Hassan, commonly known as 'Afweyne', which roughly translates as 'Big Mouth'. He was the driving force behind dozens of hijackings over a period of several years, most famously the notorious attack on the massive *Sirius Star*. Establishing bases in pirate coastal havens such as Eyl, Harardhere and Hobyo, Big Mouth had an incredible run of multimillion-dollar successes. In his own country, he became something of a cult figure. But his business empire extended beyond piracy, with many fingers in many pies in several countries. His fame spread further afield too. In Libya, Colonel Gaddafi praised him as some sort of Muslim hero, invited him on a state visit and feted him for several days of celebrations.

The only thorn in Big Mouth's side was Al-Shabaab, the militants who were now in control of much of southern Somalia. They saw how much money he'd been making and demanded $100k per hijack as 'protection money'; a guarantee not to interfere in his operations.

Several countries issued arrest warrants and tried to apprehend Big Mouth, but he always seemed to evade capture. Since Somalia was a country riddled with corruption and Big Mouth had friends in high places, he seemed to be almost untouchable. Then, in 2013, he held a press conference to announce that not only was he retiring from piracy but was also trying to persuade many of his partners in crime to do the same. A Road To Damascus moment? A sudden seeing of the light? It's more likely that the increasing use of maritime security guards like me had made hijacking a tougher proposition and he wasn't making so much lolly anymore. Time to diversify and concentrate on his other business interests.

He even persuaded the new federal Somali government to give an amnesty for contrite pirates and to fund rehabilitation programmes to help them learn new skills. Noble-sounding stuff, but Big Mouth still had an eye for a quick buck; offering the release of all hostages still held by the various piracy gangs in return for a couple of million dollars, a deal which never materialised.

But the countries whose ships had fallen into the hands of the 'pirate king' in the past few years hadn't forgiven or forgotten the trouble and expense he'd caused them. They were still out to silence Big Mouth, ideally by putting him behind bars. And at the end of 2013, they managed it. The various international arrest warrants hadn't worked, so they had to come up with something a bit more devious. Appealing to his vanity, they lured him into flying to Brussels to take part in a film documentary about his daring adventures on the high seas. But it was a sting. The Belgian authorities promptly arrested him and put him on trial for the hijacking of a Belgian ship several years before. He got 20 years in prison; the first pirate chief to be put in the dock by the rest of the world. Sadly however, they couldn't touch any of his ill-gotten gains.

A different sort of 'pirate king' was Abdullahi Abshir, known as 'Boyah'. No smart suits and silk shirts here. Boyah had once been a lobster-diver from the coastal village of Eyl, until the illegal fishing-fleets had ripped up the reefs and destroyed the lobster breeding-grounds. It's reckoned he was the driving force behind several dozen pirate attacks and big-ransom hijacks. Like Big Mouth, Boyah was unrepentant about his activities, summoning up that old chestnut that he and his men were no more than 'coastguards', defending their homeland from evil outside forces, among whom he seemed to include the international forces of *Operation Atalanta* and the *Combined Task Force 151*. He was a cocky bugger too, claiming that his men had hijacked ships right under the very noses of the naval forces and that nothing was going to stop their activities. He also hinted that the authorities onshore, however much they condemned all this in public, were actually in cahoots with the 'coastguard' and that they took a healthy slice of the ransom money.

Somalia is an assembly of several regions, often very different in character; in some ways, not unlike the structure of Great Britain.

In the story of piracy, the most important of these is called Puntland. Making up about a third of greater Somalia, Puntland is its northern-most region, with two long coastlines on either side of the Horn of Africa; one on the Gulf of Aden, the other on the Indian Ocean. It is this endless, isolated seaboard, dotted here and there with little, half-hidden harbours, which made Puntland the perfect pirates' nest in the first decade of the 21st century.

In 1998, several years after the Somali Civil War had

broken out, Puntland had declared itself a semi-autonomous state. Like Scotland or Wales, this allowed it to be, to some extent, its own boss. It also enabled it to ring-fence itself somewhat from the very worst of the troubles that were tearing apart the rest of Somalia, especially in the terrorist-infested south. But this greater degree of stability couldn't ring-fence it from the curse of piracy. Quite the opposite in fact.

The 'Land of Punt', as it had once been known, had been a trading nation since the days of the ancient Egyptians. But its glory days were long gone. It is a largely arid, semi-desert region of around four million people, over two-thirds of whom are aged under 30. And jobs were hard to come by. In its largest city, Bossasso, some work could be found in the dockyards, but in smaller towns and villages like Garowe, Eyl and Harardhere, things were a whole lot tougher. Yet, compared with the rest of Somalia, it could still be said to function and in the glory years of piracy, Puntland was the home of the pirate kings.

It was also the place where the land-based aspects of the pirates' business were in full swing. The pirates only made money when their ransoms were paid by the owners of the hijacked ships. Until then the vessels and their crews were costing them money. To minimise this, everything was run like a very slick military operation and every man had his role to play. There were all sorts of fixers, agents and businessmen involved in the necessary transactions. And on one occasion, I found myself among them.

The PMSC which was my current employer was acting on behalf of a ship owner and its negotiators who were involved in a hijack and ransom scenario. I was asked to escort a cash payment to a Puntland businessman who was negotiating on the pirates' side. I'd always been intrigued by what went on behind the scenes after a vessel had been hijacked, so I was keen not to miss the chance to witness this piece of the kidnap and ransom jigsaw.

Essentially the mission was pretty straightforward. I was to be the bodyguard to a big dollop of wonga and make sure it was delivered safely to the right person. Simple right? What could go wrong?

I was to be one of a pair. My colleague and I took a plane to Oman then on to Yemen. In the port of Aden, we picked up a small rucksack, secured by a strong lock. Inside it was $150K. It was shown to us and carefully counted out in our presence before we signed to say we had received it. We then boarded a clapped-out Cessna and took off across the Gulf of Aden towards Puntland in northern Somalia. That old expression about flying 'on a wing and a prayer' had never seemed so apt. Sod all chance of a packet of peanuts, let alone a glass of champagne.

Somehow this knackered relic spluttered its way across the waters of the Gulf and deposited us, sweating like pigs, onto the barren airstrip at Bossasso. We were two white men in Puntland, in Somalia, and that really wasn't a great idea. Square pegs in round holes doesn't even begin to describe it. From the moment my feet touched the baked ground, all my soldier's instincts switched themselves on, all my antennae quivered in the hot, dry wind; every sudden sound, every deep shadow, every face that came too close to me.

I was pretty used to the heat, but this was indescribable,

it pounded against your forehead like a hammer and almost took your breath away. Not even an industrial-strength deodorant could have stopped your armpits and your crotch turning into Niagara Falls.

We were met by a local agent whose job it was to process us through customs. The ease with which this happened made it pretty likely that bribes had been paid to wave us through. We were treated like VIPs and no checks were made. In places like this, you didn't ask too many questions: you went in, did what you had to do, kept a low profile and got out again.

All we knew was that the money in the rucksack was part of a complicated chain of events which would eventually set free a group of innocent people. I clung to that thought all through the trip. We didn't know the name of the vessel involved or any further details; only the names of this agent and the person to whom the money was to be delivered. All we were doing was putting this piece of the jigsaw into place.

The criminal networks of the pirate kings like Big Mouth and Boyah consisted of many different groups of people – the men who attacked and captured the ship, those who guarded the hostages, those who supplied the arms and ammo, those who cooked the meals. Then there were the negotiators and the various, shadowy middle-men who oiled wheels, made things happen then disappeared back into the undergrowth.

I clutched the holdall as if my life depended on it which, in retrospect, it may have done. The local agent bundled us into a decrepit taxi which was the four-wheeled equivalent of the rust-bucket from which we'd just disembarked.

Bossasso was a big port city of about 700,000 people. It wasn't a place you'd want to rush back to, though it had pretty corners and a jumble of buildings with brightly coloured rooftops like the houses on a Monopoly board. The dusty streets were choked with traffic and heaving with people. As we slowed to a crawl in the maelstrom of the market place, I felt like a six-foot three, white-faced goldfish as curious African faces peered in at us.

Our rendezvous was at the Hurrusse Hotel, a long, low colonnaded building. In the heart of town. It was respectable enough, far from the flea-pit I'd expected, though Claridge's it wasn't. It seemed to be a major hangout for the local business community. There was lots of scurrying to and fro, doing deals in discreet corners; briefcases, files and parcels passing from one hand to another. As the only two Westerners, every eye was upon us, though nobody spoke. I guess we seemed like visitors from another planet, which of course is sort of what we were.

However, the Somali businessman who was the lucky recipient of the rucksack gave us an effusive welcome. Well he would, wouldn't he? We were the lottery after all; his big rollover jackpot. While we rested and drank mint tea, the rucksack was taken into a corner of the room, emptied of its contents and every single banknote counted. I watched as the fat wads of paper gradually covered the table. You could almost smell them.

Once he was satisfied that we'd not nicked so much as a fiver to buy an ice-cream, all sorts of paperwork was bandied to and fro. The whole palaver took the best part of three hours, during which I felt almost as vulnerable as I had in Iraq or out on the ships with a pirate skiff firing at

Clockwise from top left: 11 years old playing for primary school and being picked up by the Preston North End Centre for Excellence (front row, left); Aged 9, a body of Baywatch and a haircut of Crimewatch, thanks Mum; With Nan, my best friend, she died while I was at sea; With daughter Evie – my greatest achievement; Mum and Dad, Mandy and David Wylie; Scoring at Fratton Park

Top: Me and my Dad before our annual march through Blackpool on Remembrance Day.
Far right: My father on his passing out parade in HM Royal Marines.
Right: My Dad in his annual Christmas Day Royal Marine outfit of apron and beret (also note the corps socks and belt, too)

'...he army was, next to my Dad,
...e best teacher I ever had'
...ght: With Sgt Adam Leach about
... deploy on operations.
...elow: On patrol in Al Amarah,
...aq, 2005.

Above: myself with the late Jon Neve, 'a soldier of
outstanding qualities.' On day 1 of army training.

'Within 48 hours of Alan's death, we were reluctantly out
on patrol again, travelling on the very same routes'
Left: LCpl Alan Brackenbury, who tragically lost his life on
29th May 2005 in Al Amarah, Iraq.
Below: Squadron Sgt Major WO2 Alex Rutter and
A Squadron SNCOs, pay their final respects to LCpl
Brackenbury, Al Amarah, Iraq 2005.

Above: It was the sheer size of modern merchant vessels which was to make them such an easy target. Gentle giants whos responses were slow and lumbering. All of this was good news for anyone who wanted to attack them...
Below: Armed Somali pirates prepare a skiff in Hobyo, northeastern Somalia, ahead of attacks on ships. January 2010.

Right: A week in Dubai waiting for another ship, another dip in a sun-drenched swimming pool...
Below: Dick the Dummy shortly before going 'Man Overboard' off the coast of Yemen

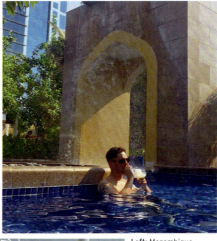

Left: Mozambique Channel 2011, monitoring a pirate action group after a suspicious approach
Below: A wooden fabricated AK47 that one of the crew members made for an unarmed transit in 2010, not much use in a real fire fight but sometimes it was enough to avoid one

Left: Filming with HBO/VICE for a documentary on pirates, floating armouries and private contractors, Horn of Africa 2016.

Above: Briefing the officers of a vessel on what to do in the event of a Code Red situation. **Right:** With Dave McFarland test-firing weapons before entering High Risk Area. **Below:** Me with Nathan Burns in the Gulf of Aden 2010.

Top left: With one of the crewmen I was locked in the Citadel with in 2010.
Top right: Maritime security operations on the west side of Africa, where a very real threat remains today from pirates and armed criminals, pictured here with Nigerian security forces, 2013.
Left Alongside the ship's captain and Rocky Mason, Mozambique Channel 2011.
Below: Counter Piracy training for Djibouti Coast Guard, Horn of Arica.

Jordan Wylie,
Ambassador, Chennai 6 Campaign

Left: At the UN HQ. I was invited to talk on counter piracy issues in the Indian Ocean.

Above: I am proud to be an ambassador for the Chennai 6 Campaign, helping the families of six former British servicemen who have been jailed in India, in what the maritime industry believes is a huge miscarriage of justice.

Below: 'In this life, you can't ever go backwards. You can choose to stay still, to tread water, but that's not for me. So the only way is forward, whatever it might bring. However strong you think you are, you can never know what's coming at you out of a clear blue sky.'

me. I wanted out of there and fast. This country wasn't a place for us.

But in the end we got away with it. We didn't bother to stop for that ice-cream or to buy any souvenirs for the mantelpiece back home. We got our arses back to that scorched, arid airfield, crossed ourselves and climbed back into the geriatric Cessna. Never have I been so glad to feel the wheels fold up into the fuselage and to see an airport runway vanish beneath me. Hot, bothered and buffeted by the winds over the Gulf, we finally bumped down onto the airstrip at Aden. When, on a decent plane that offered both peanuts and champagne, we saw Oman again, it felt like arriving in Shangri-La.

It had been a worrying trip, not just from a physical perspective but also from a legal standpoint. Many countries around the world had laws that prohibited any engagement in practices like the ransom process, with many governments flatly refusing to authorise any payments to 'terrorists'. This was for many reasons, but mainly because it might encourage them in planning and equipping further operations.

But terrorism and piracy were not the same thing. There was a world of difference between paying a pirate, who was essentially a criminal, and paying a terrorist. The first was perfectly lawful, the second was emphatically not. But though both the UK and USA governments had accepted there was no substantive link between piracy and terrorism in Somalia, you still had to be a bit careful. Luckily for me, the PMSC I was working for had engaged a highly reputable law firm which took compliance and regulatory issues very seriously and also played a very important role in the release process. But if you didn't understand all the regulations and legalities surrounding these issues, or if you found yourself employed by a 'cowboy' company, you could end up in serious trouble or even spend the rest of your days in a foreign jail.

In a comfy bed in my air-conditioned room in Oman I vowed that, for myself and for the ones I loved, I'd never again take a risk like that. But then I got to thinking about other people's loved ones too. The loved ones of the men held hostage on that ship, the names of which I'd never know. If what I'd just done had played even a small part in bringing those frightened families back together again, maybe I'd done a good job after all. The trouble was that I'd never really find out.

But at least I could now say I'd been into Puntland, the home of all these guys who'd taken their skiffs onto the high seas and caused havoc to the nations of the world. Even the briefest glimpse of it had somehow given me a sense of why they were doing what they did. It was a country pared down to the bone by poverty, deprivation and war. A country with its nerve-ends exposed. Somalia was not a place where you wanted to linger for long.

CHAPTER 11

First Assault

It happened just as I'd imagined it a million times. Without warning. That small white dot on the radar screen, that speck of dandruff moving ever closer. Shit.

I felt the tightening in my stomach, the thump of my heart, the sweat on my forehead, as hundreds of men had done before me. Now we'd see how our defences held up, how effective the training we'd given the crew. It was mid-2010. I'd been a maritime security guard for nearly six months without so much as a sniff of a pirate. I'd got to the stage where I would have been less surprised to see Moby Dick coming at me across the waves. But this was it mate. Rehearsals were over; it was show-time. Jesus. Here we go.

The ship was the *Sea Wolf,* a dry bulk carrier, her giant holds stuffed with iron ore. She was a fairly new ship, nearly 1,000 feet long, weighing over 90,000 tons. She sailed under the flag of the Marshall Islands, but her crew was mostly Indian. It was one of the longer transits, all the way across the Indian Ocean from Sri Lanka to Saudi Arabia and back again. I was glad to have my old mate Macca McFarland beside me as my number two, even if it meant I'd have to sit through *Sweet Caroline* yet again on karaoke night.

We'd not long entered Pirate Alley when, in the wee small hours of the morning, the phone rang in my cabin. It was Macca on the bridge.

'Trouble Jord,' he said quietly. 'You'd better get up here.'

Sure enough, there they were on the radar. Two dots about six nautical miles away. I reminded myself that nautical radars were far from infallible. The dots could well be wave crests. They could also be fishing boats, except that fishing boats tended to be either stationary or moving in a straight line. But these two dots were moving erratically and that was dead suspicious. Even more worrying was the fact that they were coming from behind us, towards the freeboard at the stern, that vulnerable lowest point where it was easiest to vault aboard. I'd been worried about the freeboard; there had been a cock-up with the supply of razor-wire and we'd not had enough to totally protect it. Damn and blast.

Yet the timing was odd. It was a dark night. No moonlight. Pirates tended to attack either at dawn or dusk, when it was murky enough to provide some cover, but still light enough to see by. At this point, the crew I'd posted on the bridge-wings as supporting watchmen for my security team, still couldn't see a thing. Maybe it was Moby Dick after all. And Mrs Moby Dick.

When I reached the bridge, I instantly realised there was a problem beyond what was on the radar screen. The Indian captain was flapping.

'He's losing it Jord,' Macca had whispered.

'The last thing we need,' I replied

With the possible exception of scabies, nothing spreads as fast as panic. Especially when it comes from the person who's supposed to be in control. People think that if he's scared, they have every reason to be too. Already I could see it in the eyes of the officers and crew on the bridge. When you're a leader of people in the military or the master of a vessel at sea, you have to stay cool, calm and collected. Nobody's saying that's easy. You may well be as petrified as anyone else, but you just can't let it show and communicate it to others, that's all. I used to call it the 'swan effect'; serene on the surface, but shitting yourself underneath. But projecting that serenity was everything.

'We must stop the ship!' said the captain.

It was as if he'd already decided all was lost and that we might as well invite any attackers on board and offer them a cup of tea and a biryani.

'I'm not sure that's the best option, sir,' I replied politely. 'It would only make it easier for them.'

I realised now that it was up to me to take control without ever, for even one split second, appearing to do so. I must never weaken the perception that the captain was God on his ship. I could only advise; the ultimate decisions must be his.

Unfortunately, my next piece of advice was hard for him to swallow.

'I think we should black her out sir,' I said.

'That's illegal Mr Wylie! ' he snapped back. 'Against every rule of the sea.'

'I know that sir.'

'This is a new ship. It cost millions of dollar to build. Do you want us to collide with some other vessel and cause huge damage, even loss of life? I could end up in jail.'

'If we were to be hijacked and held to ransom sir, the price might be far higher than any possible damage,' I replied. 'And I'm suggesting it to save lives, not to risk them.

I believe that the risk justifies the action.'

'*All* the navigation lights off?'

'All of them sir. Out of sight, out of mind.'

And so the ship plunged itself into total darkness and ploughed on through the pitch-black waters of the Gulf.

By now, we were in a 'stand-to'. The other two guys on the team had been dragged from their bunks and were with Macca and me on the bridge.

'Let's unlock the armoury now please,' I said.

I thanked my lucky stars that, if this was going to be my first encounter with pirates, this voyage was a fully armed transit. Macca and the guys went to retrieve the weapons from their secure storage place. These 'controlled goods' were kept as close to the bridge as a captain would allow, but always firmly locked away in the ultra-strong 'Peli-cases' used by the military. It was vital that the crew, untrained in weaponry, must never be able to access them under any circumstances. If some bloke flipped his lid over the quality of the breakfasts, you couldn't have him blowing the cook's head off. For safety, ammunition was always stored separately but nearby. Luckily, we had close to the ideal of 200 rounds of ammo.

The sight of the guns did nothing to help chill the captain and crew. Nor did the moment when we put on our helmets and body armour. I could smell the fear, barely contained. It was vital that the four of us stayed totally calm, totally professional.

Then Macca called me over to the radar.

'Look, Jord' he said quietly. 'There's a third dot. Bigger than the other two. Moving much slower than the smaller ones. You know what that means, don't you?'

'Yeah. Shit.'

All hope of the dots just being wave crests was now gone. There was little doubt that the two smaller dots were pirate skiffs and the bigger one was the mothership from which they'd embarked.

Suddenly we saw a flash of light out there in the darkness. It could have been a torch on one of the skiffs. We just didn't know. But it confirmed that somebody was out there and that the *Sea Wolf* was being hunted down.

'I think it's *Code Yellow* time sir,' I said to the captain.

'You're sure Mr Wylie?' he asked.

'Sure, sir,' I replied. 'And right now.'

All over the ship, the Tannoy cut into seafarers' dreams. Clothes were swiftly pulled on. Precious possessions, pictures of wives and kids, were stuffed into pockets. Everyone mustered at the prearranged place below decks. And deep down in the guts of the ship, the Citadel was ready and waiting.

There was no longer much point in trying to hide the *Sea Wolf*. I now advised the captain to end the blackout and increase the speed of the ship. The huge black shadow of the vessel was pin-pricked with light again. But now I needed more illumination than just the navigation lights could provide. I wanted to see what we were up against with my own eyes. I asked the captain's permission to fire a warning flare from the bridge wing. The thing flew up into the night sky and, for its brief life, lit up the sea around us as if it were midday. With my night-vision monocle, I swept the seas beyond the stern and there, sure enough, no more than a mile off and closing fast, was a skiff with three or four men on board.

Now they knew that the ship was aware of their presence and on its guard. What they still had no way of knowing was what its defences were, what retaliation they could expect to face.

The order went down to the engine-room to speed up. Except it wasn't like putting your foot down on the accelerator of a car. This was 90,000 tons of iron and steel. It took time. But gradually, under my feet, I could feel the power of her massive engines thrusting us faster across the water. It was unlikely that we could outrun the pirate skiffs but we might as well make things harder for the bastards.

'Load the weapons please,' I told the team.

I gave the instruction as casually as possible, as if I were asking them to pass the salt. Tensions were high on the bridge now. People trying to stay cool but silently aghast at what was happening. Remember that the chances of falling victim to an attack were still statistically low. It was something that might happen to somebody else but not to you. But now, here it was. Right in your face. In the middle of a calm ordinary night, you had woken up to find yourself in the nightmare.

The magazines were fitted into the guns, but there was no question of firing just yet. International maritime law clearly stated that before you engage you must be bloody sure that your ship and, more importantly, the lives of your crews are definitely threatened. Just because something comes close to you, it isn't necessarily hostile. It could just be a fishing-boat or some other harmless vessel. If you fired too soon and killed a few innocent souls, you stood a good chance of spending a very long time in some hellhole prison while the rats nibbled at your toes. (A year or so later, this would be exactly what happened when marines working as guards on an Italian oil tanker *Enrica Lexie* shot and killed two Indian fishermen, believing them to be pirates. This became a major diplomatic crisis between Italy and India and the marines were imprisoned for several years.)

But few innocent fishing boats ever travelled at speeds like this. On the radar screen, the dots were rapidly closing in on our stern. Three-quarters of a mile. A half. A quarter. Increasing our speed hadn't helped much. *Sea Wolf* was a fucking inappropriate name for a vessel like this. Elephant or snail would have fitted better. How many minutes would it be before the first rocket-propelled grenade came roaring out of the dark and punched a bloody great hole into the captain's spanking new ship?

'Captain, whoever they are, we need to send these guys a message.'

'What's that, Mr Wylie?'

'That this ship has security on board and that we're armed,' I replied. 'I suggest we fire some warning shots. Let's see if we can scare them off.'

He seemed reluctant but agreed.

From the bridge-wing, Macca released a couple of rounds towards the stern and up into the sky. We crouched down, waiting for a response from the darkness. It didn't come. The only sound was the churning of the engines as we hurtled over the waves. Inside the bridge itself, nobody spoke. Everyone stood stock-still, dealing with his private thoughts. We held our breath. Then the silence was broken.

'They've turned around!' shouted the officer scanning the radar.

Sure enough, the two smaller dots were moving away

from us and back towards the third, larger dot. Over the next 10 minutes, we watched as the skiffs then melted into the mothership which then slowly drifted off the radar screen.

It was over. At least for now. *Code Yellow* was now revoked. In a sense, the crew, mustered below decks, had been in the worst position. At least up on the bridge we'd known what was going on; down below, they'd had to deal with uncertainty and the possibility that the ship was about to be hijacked. Now they could go back to bed. The photos of loved ones which they'd grabbed in the first panic could be put back beside their bunks. But it was unlikely that anyone would sleep much tonight.

'Thanks to you and your team Mr Wylie,' said the captain. 'Good job.'

'Thank you sir.'

The order was given to slow the ship down. Gradually, the pulse of the engines lessened beneath my feet. The *Sea Wolf* breathed easy again.

And what did I feel? Mixed emotions. Relief that the pirates had fled and that everyone was safe. There were no dead bodies on the decks. Not so much as a scratch on her spanking new paintwork. But I'd be fibbing if I claimed that there wasn't also a slight sense of anticlimax. After all the risk-assessment, the planning and the training, I guess I'd really wanted to see how I'd cope when it came to the real thing.

The toughest thing in the army had always been the long periods of boredom between the short bouts of engagement. Now, in my new career, I'd recognised that old problem once again, that irritating twitch for something exciting to happen. I had to remind myself sharply that the name of this game was deterrence, chasing away those who wanted to do us harm and that tonight we'd achieved exactly that. Not, repeat not, covering myself in any sort of glory. The medal my team had won tonight was seeing the relief in the faces of the crew, watching them go gratefully back to their beds, thanking whichever god they worshipped. Still, it would've been good to have at least seen the whites of the pirates' eyes.

Of course, there was no guarantee that they wouldn't come back again and perhaps in greater strength. There had been more than one incident where this had happened. For the next day or two, I doubled the watchmen on the bridge-wings.

So why had the pirates turned tail so easily? My guess was that their approach was opportunistic; in other words that they had indeed been, ironically, just out on a 'fishing-trip'. Various websites would've told them exactly what prey was available that night and they'd come out to see what their chances might be. It probably hadn't been planned in much detail; if it had, we might not have got off so easily. It was a bit like a bunch of lads hitting the town on a Saturday night, hoping for some trouble. But once they'd discovered the *Sea Wolf* had armed security on board, they'd decided the trouble might be too much to handle.

In short, the whole incident was a textbook justification for the use of armed protection on merchant ships. And unlike lots of security guards who only ever had uneventful transits, at least I'd now actually seen a bloody pirate. I was no longer a virgin.

I was also pleased that all my guys had performed so

well. Pros to their fingertips. I was proud to be their leader.

'Hey, it's karaoke tomorrow night, Jord,' said Macca as he headed for his cabin.

'*Sweet Caroline?*'

'Well yeah. This lot haven't heard me do it yet.'

'Beam me up Scottie,' I said.

CHAPTER 12

Grabbing For The Ladder

A knock on my cabin door.

'Hey Jord, what you doing in there? Give it a rest mate or you'll go blind.'

'Piss off Rocky,' I shouted back from my bunk. 'Don't judge others by yourself.'

'There's a new DVD going round the ship,' he called through the door. 'A real three-hanky job apparently. Want me to get hold of it for you?'

'I'm reading a book actually, Rocky.'

'Yeah right mate.'

I could hear his laugh fade away along the corridor.

'Jord's locked away in his cabin again. Dirty bastard,' he'd tell the other guys.

But stretched out on my bunk, I *was* reading a book. A pile of them in fact. And not one contained so much as a single nipple.

There wasn't that much free time on the ships. For both the security teams and the crews, most of it was spent sleeping, eating or taking endless showers in the sub-tropical heat. What was left after that, many guys just frittered away; playing video games or locked inside their iPods. If the ship was big enough, there might be a small gym, where the gym-bunnies like my mate Dave Cunliffe would spend every possible minute throwing dumbbells around.

But at least both Dave's bulging biceps were the same enormous size. It was a standing joke that most seafarers had one bicep bigger than the other, depending on whether he was left or right-handed. It's no exaggeration to say that the invention of the DVD had brought innocent pleasure to hundreds of thousands of lonely, frustrated blokes all over the world. Many would have put it right up there with the wheel and the internal combustion engine as an object which had brought the most benefit to mankind.

'Honestly mate, you ought to get a hobby,' I once said to a bloke famous for the hours he spent in his cabin with a box of Kleenex.

'It *is* my hobby,' he replied.

I'm not saying I never indulged, but I still had that old horror of wasting time. By now, I could see my 30th birthday on the horizon. My army career was finished forever. There was no going back to that. This new chapter of my life was to be make or break for Jordan Wylie. I just didn't have time to be *any* sort of wanker.

Right from my earliest transits, I'd sensed that I might just be the right guy in the right place at the right time. However classy their pedigree in other aspects of security might be, few people had any direct experience of counter-piracy work. It was the blind leading the blind. Pretty soon, anyone with any track-record whatsoever became a hot property and I quickly found myself as one of those guys. By the time the Gold Rush really hit its height, I was nearly always the Team Leader of a three or four-man team. I nearly always got along with people and I worked hard to earn their respect and their confidence. Suddenly I had the status that my back injury had deprived me of in the army. I'd be lying if I pretended that it didn't feel good. I often thought back to that villa in Doha and Daz Knight demanding to know who the fuck I thought I was. In a way, he'd been right of course. At that point, I'd not known the arse from the elbow of a ship. But now, nobody asked me that question any more.

In some ways, it was a weird existence, schizophrenic even. I was flying backwards and forwards between two totally different lives. The first in cool grey England, mowing the grass, emptying the dishwasher, visiting friends on a Sunday afternoon. In that cosy world, about the worst thing that could happen was not finding the right kind of cabbage in Sainsburys. The other life was under a sub-tropical sun, living in a tiny cabin, on constant lookout for danger and perhaps even death, zooming at you across the waves.

But getting home to the UK was becoming increasingly difficult. Even basic communications with home were tricky. Except on the largest, most sophisticated ships, there was no Wi-Fi and even then you'd need to get the captain's permission to send an email. The security team had a satellite phone but that was for emergency use only and it wasn't a good idea to use up its juice just to call your mum on her birthday. When we got into a port, we'd buy local SIM cards for our mobiles but the signals were sometimes dodgy so it was often hit-and-miss. After my years away in the army, my partner and my parents were used to not hearing from me for weeks on end, but now I was away from home far more than I ever had been in the forces. A couple of times, I was away for nearly three months.

But hey, the money was still rolling into the bank. A month-long voyage round the Indian Ocean could put £20k in my pocket. Within a year of leaving the army and going on my first voyage, we had enough in the bank to get a mortgage on a house in Andover; an unimaginable dream not so long ago. Now I could buy designer clothes, expensive meals, nice holidays. Laura and Evie wanted for nothing – except for my being there and living like most other families did. I was missing out on the thousand little pleasures of seeing Evie grow from a baby into a toddler. When I did get home, she sometimes didn't seem to know who this stranger was and clung to her mother. There's a price to be paid for everything in this life.

It seemed to be an unsolvable problem. If you rushed back to the UK at the end of every job, you could lose out on work. For the Private Maritime Security Companies, it was always quicker and cheaper to hire a guy already in the Middle East or East Africa, rather than fly somebody out from Britain. However this meant putting us up in hotels and letting us loaf around the pool for a few days till the transit was ready. Before long, I'd become a slightly spoiled authority on the five-star billets of Dubai, Mauritius, the Maldives and the Seychelles. The volcanic ash-cloud that caused the shutdown of most of Europe's airspace in April 2010 and stranded millions of travellers, left me and my mates stuck for a whole week in a posh Cairo hotel. Well, I'd always wanted to see the pyramids and the Sphinx. Every cloud has a silver lining. After a while though, some companies economised on hotel costs and bought villas in the various port cities where their teams could stay. It wasn't any sort of come-down. With swimming pools, maids to clean and cooks to feed us, these places were the poshest barracks I'd ever been in. It was a very nice existence indeed.

Apart from my increasing worry about the time I was away from home, I had little to moan about. But as I crossed and re-crossed the Gulf of Aden and the Indian Ocean, where was I actually heading? Anywhere worth going?

It was on one of these lonely night-shifts on the bridge-wing, staring out into the darkness, that the thought first struck me like a slap in the face. I couldn't believe it hadn't hit me before. What would happen if guys like me actually succeeded in driving the Somali pirates off the water and the Gold Rush was eventually over? Would I be beached too? What would I do? Home to the UK with limited prospects and the money slowly trickling out of the bank? Back in the Tesco car park lifting and lowering that barrier? Jesus, no way. But yes Jordan, I told myself, that's exactly what could happen. Unless somehow, you build on what you're doing now. Unless you make sure that the foothold you've now got in the security game can lead you up the ladder. Invest in your future mate or you're screwed.

So, in those little ship's cabins, hot as hell if the aircon was buggered and with the smell of my roommate's socks in my nostrils, I began to investigate exactly what the rungs of that ladder might be and how I could climb them. The obvious route was to build on the foundation course on Security and Risk Management which I'd done back in the army. While the rest of the guys were blasting Coldplay into their ears or playing table tennis, I started on the road towards a BA Hons in the same subject. They all took the piss of course, but I wasn't bothered.

The more I studied, the more I convinced I became that

I'd picked the right ladder to climb. Though piracy was the most dramatic and, to the wider world, the sexiest element to it, maritime security was quickly becoming a much wider field. Apart from the protection of merchant shipping, it began to involve areas like people-trafficking, drug-dealing, illegal fishing and, above all, terrorism. Security challenges were becoming ever more complex. The Gulf of Aden and the Indian Ocean were no longer just threatened by piracy for ransom, but also by terrorist activity. It was a double whammy. These dangerous waters became more dodgy almost by the day.

All of this meant that the opportunities for experienced professionals like me could become ever broader. Even if Somali piracy did eventually end, my new qualifications meant I'd be well-placed to keep on climbing up that ladder. Of course, it's not good to think that conflict and tragedy for some can create chances for others, but sadly that's the truth of it. The world is shit sometimes.

In the meantime though, my life on the ships continued to be as valuable as any piece of paper from a university. Unlike land-based security where you're usually working in just one country, travelling to and fro across the seas took you into many countries. Countries with different laws, cultures and attitudes, so I was always learning how to reboot my behaviour from one to the other. The Arab nations were the most tricky; expecting western visitors to conform to their ways whereas the African states, many of them former British colonies, tended to be more flexible and easier to deal with.

As the saying goes, knowledge is power. Whether it comes from a posh degree or just from knowing how to talk to, and respect, a Yemeni lady or the Filipino who cooked my breakfast. Gradually, for the first time in my life, I began to feel that I did have power. The power to control my own destiny. Till now, as a boy from an ordinary street in a deprived town, never expected to be more than factory-fodder or a low-ranking soldier, I'd somehow accepted that I'd always be under the authority of somebody else. Saluting, clicking my heels, snapping to attention for the rest of my days. That old 'three bags full sir' crap. Well maybe Jordan Wylie could do a hell of a lot better than that. Maybe anything was possible after all.

CHAPTER 13

The Big Bang

Just as the *Sea Wolf* hadn't been exactly wolf-like, the *Ocean Beauty* wasn't remotely beautiful. Nor, unlike the former vessel, did she have the compensating grace of being brand spanking new. Yet another dry bulk carrier, she was a good 20 years old by the time I was posted aboard her soon after my adventure on the *Sea Wolf* and she wasn't ageing particularly well. A wrinkly old girl if ever there was one. Sod all chance of a Jacuzzi on this trip.

Though she sailed under a Hong Kong flag, was captained by a Pakistani and crewed by a melting-pot of ethnicities, the *Ocean Beauty* was owned by a big American shipping line. We were sailing from the port of Salalah in Oman all the way down to Dar es Salaam in Tanzania. This meant that not only did we have to cross the very centre of Pirate Alley, we also had to go perilously close to Socotra, an island which belonged to Yemen but was positioned about 150 miles off the tip of Somalia.

Socotra was extraordinary; a bit like the 'lost world' of Arthur Conan Doyle, with soaring mountains rising out of the sea, limestone caves and incredible species of flora and fauna dating back 20 million years, many of them found nowhere else on the planet. Bizarrely shaped tree trunks looked like alien creatures from a movie. You'd not have

156

been totally surprised to see a velociraptor peeking at you from behind a bush. But the island was a bit scary in more ways than one. Since the outbreak of piracy, Socotra had quickly become notorious as a forward operating base where pirates could plan their assaults, stockpile their weapons and store fuel for their boats. In short, it was a place that required a wide berth. But on some journeys that just wasn't realistic. And this was one of them.

So there we were. No weapons and sailing too fucking close to a pirate-haven. Luckily, my team was made up of some first-class operators. Rob Davies was a former NCO in the Household Cavalry, who'd been injured in Iraq. From Newcastle with a strong Geordie accent, he was a fund of funny stories from his colourful life; the best possible companion on the bridge-wing. Lee Wallis and Willy Williamson were both fresh out of the military after multiple tours of Iraq and Afghanistan and new recruits to the Gold Rush. I knew I could rely on each of them. But despite the calibre of the team, this was still a gig where I'd have to cross my fingers and think of my bank balance. The next weeks would pay for a nice little holiday for Evie or for Mum and Dad. These things were always the criteria when a job was dodgy. Anyway, we'd probably be alright.

But for the *Ocean Beauty*, disillusion came not with a whimper but with a very big bang.

It was a beautiful morning, the heat not yet as intense as it would be later. We could just see the peaks of Socotra in the distance, jagged against the bleached blue sky.

We were far from alone; the radar was showered with those little white dots. You could cross the Gulf of Aden or the Indian Ocean and not spot another ship for days, but the Socotra Channel was a busy shipping-lane; we could easily see other big vessels not far away; container ships, oil tankers and bulk carriers like ourselves. Fishing-boats too and it was those you had to worry about. Not so much the larger ones, but the skiffs with their powerful outboard motors. A huge proportion of pirates had once been fishermen and they often used their old trade as a disguise for their new one. Guns, grenades, rope ladders and grappling hooks, all the paraphernalia of an assault, could so easily be hidden under a tarpaulin in the bottom of the boat. If they were approached by a patrol-boat from the Puntland Maritime Police Force or from any of the international navies, everything could be dumped over the side in seconds, the fishing-nets whipped out and sweet innocent expressions painted on their faces.

In other words, it was next to impossible to make any sort of snap judgment about the risk presented by an individual boat. You had to bide your time and monitor their behaviour. But sometimes, gut instinct had a part to play.

I was called up to the bridge by Rob Davies.

'Jord, I'm not happy about these two,' he said. 'They've been skirting round us for a while, far too close for comfort.'

I went outside on the bridge-wing and looked through the binoculars at a pair of skiffs travelling in our wake at a hell of a clip. That in itself was suspicious; few genuine fishermen were that keen to get to work. I scanned each boat for any visible evidence of 'combat indicators'; the weapons, the ladders and all the rest.

I'd just gone back in to look at the radar, when it happened.

A massive explosion. A great crash of steel and glass. A shockwave rippled through the length and breadth of the *Ocean Beauty*. A rocket-propelled grenade had been fired at us, hitting the side of the superstructure and blowing a fucking great hole. Christ, how many dead might there be?

Nobody had seen it coming, not even the lookouts on the bridge-wings. It went to show just how fast a so-called fisherman casting his nets one minute could whip out an RPG, stick the launcher on his shoulder, fire it and instantly turn himself into a pirate.

On the bridge, some people were struck dumb with shock and that included me, Rob, Lee and Willy. But others began running around like headless chickens. The captain, who'd been below at the moment of impact, came racing in with several other officers. The good news was that the grenade had struck a crew cabin which had been empty at the time but somebody's precious possessions were now in smithereens. The bad news was that I saw panic setting in, just as it had on the *Sea Wolf*. There were just too many people on the bridge now and that wasn't a good idea. At this moment, the plans and procedures which we'd carefully put in place simply hadn't kicked in. The urgent thing was to make that happen.

'Rob, we need to get control of this fast,' I said.

The usual first priority was to get the captain's permission to trigger a *Code Yellow* and muster the crew below decks. On this occasion though, the *Code Yellow* stage had effectively been leap-frogged by events. But it was important to stick to the procedures we'd taught the crew. Discipline was all important. A comfort blanket they could cling to in the midst of a bad dream.

I was peppered with questions from every direction. What the hell's happened? What shall we do? Will they fire again?

Before I could reply, the pirates provided the answer. There was a loud whoosh and another grenade flew past the windows of the bridge. Jesus.

People threw themselves onto the floor, hid behind their consoles, ducked under the chart-table. That one had missed but it had been potentially more devastating than the first. It had clearly been aimed at the bridge. Had it struck us, there would have been serious blast injuries from the glass and shrapnel flying everywhere. In a worst case scenario, all the key people on board could have been obliterated. Then who'd have steered the bloody ship?

It was the closest I'd come to death since Iraq in 2005. Maybe that was why this was the moment when my adrenaline, training and experience in war-zones suddenly kicked in. Like a mist evaporating, my head cleared of confusion, shock and fear. All at once, I was a soldier again which was what I would always be, deep in my core. Most soldiers could always rely on that moment happening, even if we couldn't always be sure exactly when. That was one of the reasons why it was the British ex-military who were so sought after in the fight against Somali piracy. We were the gold standard. I know that sounds pompous, but it's the truth.

Usually in these situations, there is an arc of escalation; a window of time between spotting a suspicious craft, judging whether or not it posed a threat and then, if it did, preparing for some sort of engagement. But not here, not now. The danger level had gone from zero to 10 in no time. This was an immediate, unexpected assault. This was flash, bang, wallop. Poor old *Ocean Beauty*.

I faced the captain.

'We're obviously under serious attack, sir,' I said.' We must act fast.'

'*Code Yellow* then?' he asked.

'*Code Yellow* sir.'

The Tannoy blasted out the necessary signal. I didn't know what was happening below decks but prayed they were now all safely mustered at the prearranged place.

I wanted the bridge immediately cleared of panicky people. The Citadel had been prepared in the engine control room. I sent one of my guys below to lead the crew to safety and make sure everyone was accounted for. With the other two, I stayed on the bridge with just the captain and the first officer. A degree of calm was restored.

'Sir, they're trying to scare us into stopping the ship so they can board,' I told the captain. 'I suggest we speed up.'

The captain looked uncertain, conflicted. It was that old issue rearing its head again. Do you stop the ship or run as fast as you can? If you stopped the ship, you hugely increased the likelihood of a boarding. On the other hand, if you ran, you might escalate the degree of violence the pirates would use to stop you. Big ships like the *Ocean Beauty* could rarely go faster than 18-20 knots, whereas pirate skiffs could easily hit 25-30 knots. They were always going to catch us, so why run? Also, if we did, it required the captain or some other competent officer to stay on the bridge to sail the vessel rather than retreating to the Citadel. That of course would make him a potential hostage in the event of a boarding which, in turn, meant that the international naval forces would refuse to make a rescue attempt, in case any crew were caught in crossfire.

But, in my view, you ran for two reasons. Firstly, to gain time to make sure everyone was in the Citadel and that our system of layered defences was as good as it could get; every door, every hatch, every staircase secured as we retreated to the safe-room. Secondly, just to make life as difficult as possible for the bastards. For me, stopping the ship would be like rolling over onto our back with our legs in the air. For most security teams, that was almost like dereliction of duty. Not to mention, fucking nuts if you were unarmed. I suddenly had visions of Rocky Mason having to jump into the sea from the *Biscaglia*. I didn't fancy the thought of doing that at all.

Ultimately though, as with everything else on board, it was the captain's decision not mine. Luckily on this occasion, he took my advice.

'Full speed ahead,' he ordered.

As the old lady took a deep breath and pushed herself forward, I activated the hoses ranged at regular intervals all around the deck. The assault had happened so fast this hadn't yet been done, but better late than never. If the water pressure was good on a ship, the sight of a dozen or more great fountains erupting into the sea could be quite a spectacular sight. Beautiful almost. Sadly, the water pressure on the *Ocean Beauty* was as geriatric as the rest of her. When the hoses were turned on, it looked like a row of old blokes with prostate problems taking a piss over the side.

We had no guns. Nor did we even have protective clothing; no body armour, no helmets. In the first years of Somali piracy, almost everything security teams really needed to fight back was in short supply. One single company in Malta was the main supplier for protective gear and there was no way they could keep up with the demand. So now, as the pirates chased us across the sea, we were dressed in polo shirts and cargo pants. It wasn't exactly like Sir Lancelot heading into the joust.

But we did have one little trick up our sleeves. Out on both the bridge-wings, we'd already placed eight rocket flares. We'd had no rocket-launchers, but a very creative bosun had found us some old steel tubes, a bit like scaffolding poles, that he let us have as makeshift substitutes. It was that old *Blue Peter* number again. John Noakes would've been proud of us. But would they work?

The first flare went off like a dream. So did the second. Then we fired the lot, one after the other, just like Guy Fawkes night. Our bark was worse than our bite of course, but it was better than nothing. Now we just had to hope that it would fool the pirates into thinking this was a ship armed to the teeth and ready to fight hard.

We couldn't answer that question right away. No further grenades hit us. No rifle shots came whizzing across the water as the *Ocean Beauty* strained every sinew to go as fast as she could. But this didn't seem to reassure the captain. He was gagging to go to the Citadel.

'I think we should hang on sir,' I replied. 'If we retreat to the Citadel, we must stop the ship and they'll almost certainly board us.'

I knew what he was thinking. He wanted to see his wife and children again. Like every seafarer, he knew all the horror stories; the fates of those many ships which hadn't had a safe-room to flee to. I wanted to see my kid again too and I reckoned that, for the moment at least, the best way to make that happen was to keep running for as long as we could.

'They haven't fired at us for 10 minutes sir,' I said. 'Let's not give up just yet.'

And so we kept going. Watching the skiffs through the binos. But keeping our heads close to cover in case another grenade should suddenly erupt in our direction. Another half an hour passed. And then, almost imperceptibly, the clear blue water between the *Ocean Beauty* and the pirate skiffs grew wider.

'Jord, I think they're turning,' said Rob.

And they were.

Just like us, the pirates didn't have the tools to do the job. We didn't have the weapons to defend ourselves, they didn't have the weapons to successfully attack and hijack us. Funny really, if the potential outcome hadn't been so serious. They'd peaked too soon, using up what they had too early in the game.

As with the *Sea Wolf*, they'd been chancers yet again; the gang of lads out looking for trouble without any definite plan. I pictured them on their skiffs as they headed back to their mothership, then home to Socotra. Effing and blinding. Bickering about who'd fired off the rocket-propelled grenades too quickly. Blaming whichever wanker back at the stores had decided they could only have so many grenades, only so much ammo. I thought back to my own grim days in the army stores, handing out the equipment. Perhaps the pirate store-keeper was some poor sod like me who'd once been a pirate but had hurt his back.

But it was a lucky escape. Plenty of 'what ifs?' What if

they'd had enough weapons for a serious assault? What if they'd not been deterred by our piss-poor hoses? What if we'd been boarded, hijacked, held to ransom?

But, for the second time, my close encounter with the pirates of Somalia had simply drifted away in the wake of the ship. Vanishing back into the nothingness from which they had come. The sea was calm again and soon the mountain-tops of Socotra, the pirate-haven, sank below the horizon. We'd escaped its clutches, but only just.

The *Ocean Beauty* headed on across Pirate Alley and south towards Dar es Salaam. Down in the crew quarters, temporary repairs had to be made to that gaping hole in the superstructure. The poor bloke whose cabin it was had to retrieve whatever he could from the wreck of his personal possessions. There would have to be a whip-round for spare underpants and socks. If the pictures of his loved ones were now shattered, at least that was better than being taken hostage and not seeing them again for months, years, or, in a worst case scenario, ever again.

CHAPTER 14

'Code Red, Code Red!'

As time went on, the pirates, and the criminals who often controlled them, got bolder. Every year, the number of successful hijacks increased. Every year, the ransoms demanded increased, even if they weren't always achieved. In the polished offices of the shipping companies, the owners and their insurers shook their heads and prayed that it would stop soon. If they'd ever been doubtful about the use of private maritime security guards on their vessels, they were rethinking that attitude pretty damn quick.

The growing cockiness of the Somali pirates was a bit like that of a fox in a city garden. Timid at first, hovering near the safety of the fence, every small prize it manages to snatch adds to its confidence, encouraging it to creep ever closer till it sticks its snout inside the kitchen door and runs off with the Sunday roast.

In August 2011, the *Jutland Star*, a chemical tanker carrying a cargo of methanol, was hijacked as it lay at anchorage just off the harbour of Salalah in Oman. It was the first vessel to be hijacked by Somali pirates within the territorial waters of another country. Brazen or what.

The *Jutland Star* had just sailed through Pirate Alley without incident. She'd had a security team on board, but they had disembarked on a service boat once the harbour had been safely reached. No shipping company wanted to pay for security for one minute longer than deemed necessary. Big mistake.

In the hectic, international anchorage of Salalah, boats of all shapes and sizes came and went at all hours. In the misty half-light of an early morning, nobody on watch on the *Jutland Star* had much bothered about the one that appeared to be loaded with cattle. Second big mistake. Hidden among the horns, the flicking tails and the piles of cow shit was a herd of pirates who managed to board the tanker without much trouble.

The pirates then ordered the ship's captain to head back across the Gulf of Aden towards Somalia. But by now, the alarm had been raised. The Omani coastguard first tried to approach her but the attackers screamed down the radio that the hostages would be killed unless they backed off. Then the Omani navy tried to intercept her, but found themselves under heavy fire. Unwilling to escalate the potential danger to the hostages, they too retreated.

With the usual pistol at the captain's head, the *Jutland Star* was then sailed, through rough monsoon weather, to the pirate stronghold of Garacad on the coast of Somalia. Here she would sit for nearly five months till a reported ransom of $10 million was paid and the 21-man Indian crew was released after their ordeal.

The sheer bloody nerve of this hijack shocked the merchant shipping world. Not only were the open seas perilous, the anchorages of non-Somali ports were now no longer safe either. The rumours flew. It had happened no more than six hours after the security team had left the ship. Bit of a coincidence. Had a local Omani shipping agent been bribed to tip off the pirates that the security team had gone? Or maybe it had been one of the coastguards? Or even someone in the Omani navy? (a bit politically sensitive if so). Could it just have been one of the so-called 'bum-boats' which buzzed like wasps round the big ships in the anchorage, selling trinkets, phone-cards and other such trivia to the bored seafarers as they waited for their berth on the dockside to become available? Had one of these alerted the pirates to the ship's sudden vulnerability? It wasn't the first or last time that these seemingly innocent peddlers were suspected of carrying out reconnaissance for the brigands. But nobody could be sure. In this part of the world, petty corruption was rife. In this case though, the result of the corruption was anything but petty. It was a security cock-up of gargantuan proportions.

The *Jutland Star* wasn't an only child. She had a sister called the *Jutland Queen* and it was to this vessel that my team and I were swiftly sent only a week or so after her twin had been hijacked. The ship owners, by now involved in tense negotiations to release the first ship, were nervous as cats about any assault on the rest of their large fleet. There must be no more security lapses. The route of the *Jutland Queen* was to be straight through Pirate Alley to Djibouti, the small state on the coast of the Gulf of Aden, immediately to the north of Somalia.

Our deployment was a right old rush. The team gathered quickly together in Sri Lanka and was ferried about 20 miles out into the Indian Ocean to the ship. All my guys were the best of British. Nathan Burns, Dave Cunliffe and Jeff Seery.

On the service launch that took us out to the ship was a

young Sikh guy, much the same age as me. He sat alone in a corner, apart from the rest of us. Smartly dressed, wearing an immaculate black turban, he seemed distracted, as if the weight of the world was on his shoulders. I imagined he was a new crew member, perhaps even a third officer. I tried to chat, but he didn't seem interested, answering me in monosyllables. At first, I think he thought we were just the service launch crew, but eventually asked who we were. I explained that we were the security team, going out to protect the ship.

As we approached the ship, the crew was lined up along the rails. The freeboard was quite low, so I could see their faces and hear their voices.

'Good evening, captain sir,' one called out.

'Good evening crew,' someone near me replied.

Shit. It was the young Sikh sitting beside me. This was the new commander of the *Jutland Queen* I exchanged glances with the other guys on the team. We sensed at once this wasn't going to be an easy gig.

Naturally, every seafarer on board the *Jutland Queen* was painfully aware of what had only just happened to their sister ship. At this point, nobody even knew where the hijacked ship actually was; she'd literally vanished from the radar. Possibly, most of them knew somebody who was now a frightened hostage. A good friend, perhaps even a brother. I wondered how many wives, girlfriends and mothers had tried to persuade their menfolk not to make this trip. On the *Jutland Queen*, everybody was tense.

Unfortunately the most tense of them all seemed to be the new captain. It turned out that this was his very first command. Our first glimpse of the vessel had been his, too. The ship was totally strange territory to him as were the men now under his authority. So he had a lot to cope with. And now there was a high-level risk of pirate attack. Absolutely the last thing he needed.

The second last thing was having to deal with a security team. He'd never worked with one before and had no idea of the etiquette involved to make the relationship run smoothly. Though he was always polite, it was quickly clear that he found our presence disruptive and irritating.

As we'd leapt from the service launch onto the ship's ladder, I'd seen right away that an inexperienced captain wasn't our only problem. Despite the fact that its sister ship had just been hijacked, it was obvious at a glance that no work had been done to prepare the vessel for transiting Pirate Alley. No razor-wire. No high-pressure hoses pumped and primed for use. Jesus. I wondered what the outgoing captain had done with the BMP4 'bible' of protective measures. Lit his cigar? Used it to line the cat-litter? Unbelievable.

Normally on boarding a new ship, the first thing I'd do would be to request a private meeting with the captain and his chief officer to discuss the voyage ahead. I always liked to prepare carefully for these meetings as they were the first chance to impress them with our expertise and hopefully win their trust and confidence; vital in the event of an attack.

But this young captain had no time for me now. He was far too busy doing the handover with the outgoing captain. Not wanting to annoy him, I took the team up onto the bridge and introduced ourselves to the officers on watch, even showing them our weapons before locking them away securely. Thank Christ we were at least armed.

Then I did the fastest risk assessment of my entire time at sea. My initial impression hadn't been wrong. There was no razor-wire in place anywhere and none available on board. As on the Ocean Beauty, the pressure in the hoses was pathetic; it was prostate time again. But maybe the chief engineer could do something about that. The guys and I wandered round the decks, trying not to show how hacked-off we were. In short, the *Jutland Queen* was a sitting duck. She might as well have been tied up with a pretty pink ribbon and a gift tag that read 'To the pirates of Somalia. All yours.'

I posted Nathan on immediate watch and went to face the captain. I needed his permission to make an urgent presentation to the whole crew about security risks and to organise a drill as soon as possible. The trouble was that once the ship was moving again, we'd be entering Pirate Alley in no time and we simply weren't ready. Our relationship with the captain was non-existent, the crew couldn't be drilled to anything like the necessary level and there had been no opportunity to work out any sort of detailed plan. The guys and I felt pretty frustrated. How the hell could we be expected to do a decent job in these circumstances?

I could hardly believe that there were still many transits when we just had to cross our fingers. That went against everything I believed in. It diminished the team as experienced professionals. The issues were nearly always the same. Either, we didn't have the weapons, the ammo or the protective clothing. Or we boarded a ship and found that the basic protection measures weren't adequate or, sometimes, not there at all and it was too late to fix it. Or the captain and crew begrudged your presence and were even mildly obstructive. In this case, apart from the blessing of being armed, all of these negative boxes were ticked. Sometimes, you just felt that you were fighting with both hands tied behind your back. Yet if trouble came, you were expected, by some miracle, to be able to protect the life and limb of every soul on board that ship, not to mention the multimillion-dollar value of the ship and whatever precious cargo it might be carrying. It didn't half piss me off. End of rant.

On the *Jutland Queen*, my major comfort was the three guys on the team. All of them senior guys; operations managers in their own PMSCs who like nothing better than to get out from behind a desk and fly out to the sharp end of the business. Nathan Burns was my number two. We'd served together in the military for many years and been on the same anti-piracy jobs on many occasions. We knew pretty well what made each other tick. Throughout his army career, Nathan was known by the nickname of GWA or Ginger With Attitude, because of his curly red hair and a matching bushy beard which made him look like something from a cartoon-strip. He himself always denied he was ginger; maintaining that his hair was actually 'African sunset blond'. Like the razor-wire and the high-pressure hoses, I liked to think of him as an additional protective measure; the sight of this fearsome, flame-haired apparition being an additional deterrent to the slightly built, dark-skinned Somali pirates. He had many priceless skills; an excellent team medic, a wizard with communications and an expert at creating and preparing a Citadel. There was no safer pair of hands. If the presence of a security team was insurance for the ship owners, then Nathan Burns was insurance for any security team he worked with.

Dave Cunliffe was a big lad who liked to spend most of his time getting bigger. He had a physique like a bag of walnuts and spent most of his spare time in the ship's gym, if it had one. He came from north Wales, though his mates used to pretend they believed he was a scouser from Liverpool, which drove him up the wall. There was no easier wind-up. Dave and his pecs had been in the French Foreign Legion, one of the toughest military forces imaginable and had been involved in security work in some of the most hostile regions in the world.

My third team member was a newbie on the waves. Jeff Seery was a Scotsman who'd served as a senior non-commissioned officer in one of the Scottish infantry regiments followed by several years in Iraq as a private military contractor. Jeff and I hadn't met before but soon discovered our mutual friendship with the late Jon Neve, that irreplaceable figure from my first weeks in the army. If Jeff Seery had won Jon's friendship in the tumult of Baghdad, that was recommendation enough for me.

In the precious few hours before we entered the heart of Pirate Alley, Nathan, Dave, Jeff and I did our best to fortify this plum-target of a ship. Nathan identified the best location for a Citadel and set about equipping it and strengthening its defences. I got the chief engineer to do something about the pressure in the hoses; telling him I wanted them to piss water like a bloke who'd just drunk eight pints of lager on a Saturday night. And finally I managed to gather the crew and talk them through the drill in the event of an attack, though there was still no chance to have a proper rehearsal. 'Talking them through' was grossly inadequate and highly risky, but it was the best I could do. An extra worry, as if we needed one, was the captain's refusal to let us test-fire our weapons. He thought that gunfire might scare the crew and increase tension and fear. I understood that argument but it seemed to me totally defeated by our need to know that our bloody guns worked properly.

'Well Jord, if a shooter jams when we need it,' said Jeff, 'it'll be on his head.'

We all realised this young captain was under a lot of pressure and didn't want to deal with any more. But it was baffling that he didn't seem to appreciate the magnitude of the danger waiting for his ship in the seas she was about to enter. Incredibly, he hadn't even heard of the BMP4 protective measures. I gave him a copy of it on a USB along with some pictures of pirate attacks, a list of current pirate motherships in the area and also of the unfortunate ships, not dissimilar to his own, which were already anchored off the coast of Somalia undergoing ransom negotiations or, as in the case of the *Iceberg-1*, more or less abandoned by their owners. Was he the only man on the whole vessel who didn't know that her sister ship was sailing towards that possible fate at this very moment? Was I trying to scare him? You bet your arse I was.

As the *Jutland Queen* ploughed her way into Pirate Alley, the guys and I were extremely apprehensive, on a mental red alert. But at first, it was smooth sailing. In the brief lull, I made a renewed effort to find some common ground with the young captain. We were both much the same age. Like me, he'd clearly climbed up the ladder quite quickly. It turned out he came from the Punjab, an area I'd already visited several times, so I shared my stories with him and gradually, as the days passed, he thawed out a little, finally realising that we were there to help, not to hinder him. Maybe it dawned on him that becoming the captain of a ship which had surrendered to Somali pirates would hardly look great on his CV. Maybe putting up with a security team could be a sensible career move.

Then, as these things usually did, it came right out of nowhere. It was a calm evening, about 7pm. I always thought of this as the nicest time of day, still very warm but the fiercest, most debilitating heat had eased away. It was the monsoon season, we'd had some wild downpours and the sea was often quite rough. But tonight it was placid, with the setting sun flashing off the crests of the waves. A time to sit quietly with your own thoughts. To wonder what Laura and Evie were up to at that very moment. To picture Mum and Dad pottering in the garden or going over to visit my Nana in the house where I'd spent so much time as a kid. These moments of quiet reflection were always bittersweet. It felt good to know I was earning the sort of money my parents could never have dreamed of and that I could give my own kid the things I'd never had. But it was tough to be so far away from them. And so often. That dilemma never seemed to have an answer.

We'd just had dinner. The *Jutland Queen* was crewed largely by Indians, so the food was good, if sometimes a bit on the hot side. I stood on the deck watching the sun go down, looking out for any dolphins which might suddenly erupt from the waves. There were one or two other ships on the horizon looking, from this distance, like teeny plastic boats in a kid's bathwater. I wandered up to the bridge-wing where Nathan was on watch. Since we worked to a shift-system, you often didn't get that much time with the other guys on the team, except at the hand-over point. So it was sometimes nice to sacrifice an hour's sleep just to have a chat and a coffee. Like everyone else on board, we were all a long way from home and, just like in the army, camaraderie and a bit of banter kept up your morale. So you'd hear about how their kids were doing at school, how crap their football team was doing in the Premier League. All that stuff. The pieces of the jigsaw that make up everyone's life.

In the middle of our chat about bugger all, a young crewman called out to us from inside the bridge. Yep, you guessed. There were two dots on the radar; a few miles off. From their size, they were probably fishing boats, but one of them was skipping erratically around the edges of the lanes on the International Recommended Transit Corridor, that 'safe highway' designated to offer merchant shipping some degree of security and confidence. Genuine fishing boats just didn't move like that.

'Dodgy?' I asked Nathan as we peered at the radar screen.

'Well dodgy,' he replied, stroking the big red beard.

For the next half-hour, we kept monitoring the dots. Keeping everything crossed. But they continued to get closer. It wasn't looking good.

'Jord, they're heading directly for us,' said Nathan. 'About two nautical miles away now.'

The words had hardly left his lips when a burst of small arms fire flew in front of the *Jutland Queen*. It was literally a shot across the bows. The skiff from which it had been fired now suddenly swept in front of the ship.

'Get the shooters, Nathan,' I said.

As he raced to the weapons cupboard, the bridge filled with people. Jeff Seery appeared, groggy from his bunk where he'd been asleep after his spell on duty, no doubt dreaming of Loch Lomond. Dave Cunliffe and his pecs arrived straight from the gym, in his vest and shorts. Then of course the young captain. To my great relief, he was calm and authoritative. Maybe that tricky reserve of his would turn out to be a bonus after all. It was instantly clear he wasn't a flapper.

'With your permission sir, I suggest we trigger *Code Red* straight away,' I said.

As the alert echoed all over the ship, I silently prayed that my swift talk to the crew had been enough to make sure that panic was kept in check and that they would all move into the Citadel as smoothly as possible. Every single person accounted for. No stragglers. No dozy dickhead who'd slept through the alert.

'I want to fire a couple of warning shots, sir,' I asked the captain.' Just to show them this ship has protection and that it's armed.'

'Do it,' he replied.

I was relieved. It's amazing the effect the sound of gun-fire can have on people. Now though, another silent prayer: that the guns he'd refused to let us test would fire.

Nathan and I went out onto the bridge-wing and released a few rounds into the evening air. At the same time, Jeff took up position on the opposite bridge-wing and Dave climbed up onto the 'monkey island', the platform above the bridge which gave access to the radio and radar masts and which was the highest point on the ship. If the attackers were studying us through their binos, they'd now see four armed men ready to fight back.

The skiff which had fired the shots was still dancing around in front of our bows. The other one, which till now had kept a certain distance, came up on the port side and began small arms fire, the muzzles flashing against the sunset. All the time, both skiffs were getting closer.

'We need to fire again sir,' I told the captain, then shouted up to Dave to release two more rounds. Just as I needed the captain's authority to fire a weapon, so Dave, Nathan and Jeff needed mine.

But two rounds wasn't going to be enough. The pirates met fire with fire. This thing was escalating into a small but fierce gun battle. Dave kept on firing and I wasn't going to stop him.

The chief officer, the captain's number two and in charge of communications, had already pressed the hidden button to activate the Ship Security Alert System, notifying the shipping company that the vessel was under attack. Now he was on the radio to the UKMTO in Dubai, asking for help from the naval forces and was also in contact with the second officer who was in charge down in the Citadel, keeping him abreast of what was happening on the bridge. At this point of course, though the crew was inside the safe-room, it was not yet secured. Only when those of us left on the bridge had abandoned the fight, stopped the vessel and fled below, locking every layer of our defences behind us, could the Citadel begin to function.

But we weren't ready to do that just yet. As the gun-battle

kept going, I suggested to the captain that he start what were called 'evasive manoeuvres'. This meant steering the ship in a zigzag pattern, weaving to and fro as she crossed the water. It was a controversial practice. On the plus side, it created turbulent waves, making it harder for the skiffs to get close. On the minus, it reduced our speed, making it easier for them to catch and board us. As always, it was the captain's decision.

He decided to go for it. Through the binos, I watched the skiffs trying to cope with the instant turbulence. It was pretty hard to fire their guns, when they were bouncing around like knickers in a tumble-dryer. Then, suddenly, there was a spectacular sight. The chief engineer had done his stuff on the water pressure. Huge jets of water exploded out of more than a dozen hoses all around the decks. No dribbles now. It was eight pints of lager and no mistake. If these pirates ever managed to board us, they were going to be like half-drowned rats.

From their perspective, a ship that had looked from a distance like a pushover, must now have looked like something else altogether. A ship that was armed and ready to fight. A ship not willing to roll over with its legs in the air.

'Stop firing,' I ordered the guys.' Let's see what happens.'

The light was failing now. In these latitudes, the sun went down suddenly. Evening would turn to night in no more than a few minutes. And that was what happened now. There was no more gun fire from the skiffs. The only noise was the loud hissing of the hoses as their water evaporated into the sea.

High above the bridge, Dave and his pecs still clung on

to the 'monkey island', his AK-47 still cocked and ready. On the bridge-wings, Nathan and Jeff were the same. Inside, the captain, the chief officer and I kept our eyes on the radar. What we now saw on the screen coincided with Dave shouting down from the heavens.

'They're turning tail,' he said. 'The fuckers are running away!'

It was one of those moments when it seemed excessive to chastise him for bad language in front of the crew.

But had the danger really vanished? I told the chief officer to brief the second officer that the crew must stay in the Citadel, even if not secured, for at least another hour, till we could feel certain that the crisis had passed.

It was pitch dark by now and the radar screen stayed dark too. No dangerous dots. Eventually, the crew in the Citadel was allowed to resurface, but the whole security team stayed on the bridge for a couple more hours.

Late in the evening, I debriefed the whole crew on exactly what had occurred and praised them for their calm in the face of danger. Naturally, that calm had only been on the surface. I doubt if a single one of them hadn't believed that he was about to suffer exactly the same fate as his fellows on the *Jutland Star*.

Of course the predictable thing now happened aboard the *Jutland Queen*. All of a sudden, as if by magic, everyone became very pro-security. Even the young captain who, in the moment of crisis, had proved himself more than equal to the task of commanding a ship. I even hoped that one day I might meet him again. Things would probably be a lot different the second time around.

Despite all the obstacles the team had faced on this job,

I knew that we'd proved ourselves too. I wasn't any less grumpy that we'd had to face these hurdles in the first place, but at least we'd managed to leap them pretty damn well. 'Well done guys,' I said to the team.

As usual with ex-military men, whatever anxiety they might have felt in the tension of the moment was swiftly concealed behind a cool, 'all in a day's work' attitude.

'Nae bother,' said Jeff Seery. 'It was no worse than a Friday night in Sauchiehall Street.'

'Or Llandudno for that matter,' said Dave Cunliffe.

'Llandudno?' I said. 'But we all thought you came from Liverpool.'

'Piss off, Jord,' he said.

Before hitting the sack, I went down below to check on the Citadel. Nathan had done his usual great job in preparing it. Tonight, we'd been lucky yet again. It hadn't been needed for more than an hour. After the many transits I'd now notched up, I'd still not yet needed to flee to it, barricade the door and sit there in the dim light along with another 20 sweating, frightened souls, wondering what the next few hours, days or even months and years might bring.

How long would it be till that time arrived?

CHAPTER 15

The Lion's Den

The emails flew to and fro between me and the private security company I was working for.

'How much?'

'600 quid a day. Three-week voyage.'

'Hey, not bad. What's the catch?'

'No weapons. The ship's under a flag that doesn't allow armed guards.'

'Bugger,' I replied. 'Any other issues?'

'Well, you might think the route's a bit challenging.'

'Why? Where are we going?'

'Somalia.'

I thought he'd made a mistake, a slip of the keyboard. Or maybe he was taking the piss. But no. The round-trip voyage would start at one of the familiar ports, Salalah in Oman, heading to Mogadishu in Somalia, then south to Mombasa in Kenya and Dar es Salaam in Tanzania before crossing the Indian ocean to Karachi in Pakistan and back up to Salalah. The ship was the *Leviathan*, a dry bulk carrier carrying grain and rice as part of an international aid programme to fight the famines and deprivation endemic in some of these countries. As the name suggests, she was one of the big babes, nearly 1,000 feet long and with a weight of over 90,000 tons.

As you'll be aware by now, the first thing I did on any new gig was to make an assessment of the vessel. But sometimes, you also had to make a serious assessment of yourself. Was the reward worth the risk? Could the lolly ever compensate you and yours for what might happen to you? Every single transit across Pirate Alley carried real dangers. I was cool with that. That was the job after all. And this one was to take food supplies to people who really needed them. A job worth doing. But to go into Somalia itself? To enter the lion's den and stick my head in the lion's mouth? How many other guys had been approached, had asked if the company was having a laugh and said 'no way'? No wonder my employers were willing to pay 600 smackers a day, desperate for some dickhead like me to yield to temptation.

But bloody hell, it was a lot of dosh. Over £12K for less than a month's work. About half of what the British Army had paid me in a whole year when I was serving in Iraq. As I usually did in these situations, I thought of Alan Brackenbury and Richard Shearer. The threat of getting blown to smithereens back then had been a lot greater than the chance of copping it from any Somali pirate right now. So I took the gig and took my chances. Financially, it was a no-brainer. In every other way, it was probably fucking silly. A suicide mission even. As I was soon to find out.

Apart from going into the lion's den unarmed, I'd be going in under-manned. Instead of having the usual four-man team, they'd only been able to rustle up three of us. For both the other men, this would be their very first maritime security job. Nothing like jumping in at the deep end.

Under me was Dave Rogers, a former member of the

Parachute Regiment. Like anyone in the military with that surname he was known as Buck, after the comic-book hero. He'd worked as a private security contractor in the hostile environments of both Iraq and Afghanistan but was now eager to join the new Gold Rush. Buck was in his 40s now, divorced with kids; yet another gym bunny and built like an outside privy. A lot of his physique was decorated with tattoos and he could look quite intimidating until you got to know him. Luckily he came from Manchester, so as a pair of northerners we were on the same wavelength from the start. He was also a brilliant team medic who always carried his own extensive personal medical pack which he often used to sharpen up all the team's medical knowledge. In our job, you could never know too much about first aid.

The third on the team was Paul Riley, ex-Royal Navy. Much the same age as me, he was a quietly spoken man from Poole in Dorset. Tall and blond, he reminded me of Val Kilmer in the movie *Top Gun*. Paul had been a submariner so we joked that, if we had to go into the Citadel, he'd feel right at home being stuck in a piece of metal under the waterline with no access to the outside world.

We crossed Pirate Alley itself without incident. Then, after a few days, a thin line appeared on the horizon. Somalia. The pirate kingdom itself. It was impossible not to feel a tightening of the guts.

Words like anchorage and harbour have a nice cosy feel. They have a sense of safety. You're protected from the worst of the weather. Cheery little tug-boats will guide you in. The locals will be eager to accept your precious cargo, whatever it might be. You'll have an interesting time, seeing new sights, meeting new people from different cultures. A warm, friendly welcome awaits the weary seafarer. And when you depart, they'll all be lined up on the dockside to wish you well and wave you off.

In many ports in the volatile countries of the Middle East, this wasn't quite the vibe. In the case of Mogadishu, nothing could be further from the truth. And right now, it was often these very anchorages which presented the greatest danger – as the *Jutland Star* had discovered, hijacked from under the noses of the Omani coastguard and navy as she waited in line to unload her cargo. Anchorages are the nautical version of aircraft being stacked above an airport. Instead of planes, there are ships queueing up to be told when their berth at the dockside is ready and they can enter port to unload their cargo. Since your berth has been pre-booked, it's important that you arrive in the anchorage at the appointed time. Naturally, things can go wrong for one reason or another and so your ship stays 'stacked' for longer than you'd planned. And this is when you're vulnerable.

An anchorage off a major port is a busy place. Apart from the other large merchant ships waiting near you, there is a constant swarm of smaller craft buzzing round you: lots of fishing boats, the launches of the port authority or the police and the 'bum-boats' coming out from port to sell their fruit, fish and SIM cards to the seafarers. Any of these can easily be a cover for piracy. In short, the closer to port a merchant ship sails, the more vulnerable she becomes. A paradox really, but in these countries different rules apply. This isn't Portsmouth or Liverpool, Hamburg or Genoa. You have to switch your mind onto a different channel.

On the *Leviathan*, I had a few other reasons for apprehension. The sea was remarkably calm, flat as a mirror, the fierce sun glancing off it so your eyes were often blinded. Calm seas always makes piracy much more likely. She also had a very low freeboard, which was always a serious concern. I often wanted to get hold of the folk who designed merchant ships and bang their heads together. And, for the umpteenth bloody time, the basic protection measures were inadequate; not enough razor-wire to go round the decks; not enough high-pressure hoses to act as a visual deterrent or, if that didn't work, to sweep any intruders back into the sea.

In the five or six days before we reached Somalia, I trained the crew in basic security measures. Most were Filipino and not all spoke great English. Nevertheless, I drilled them harder than I'd ever drilled a crew on any ship before. I drilled them every day and at an unspecified time so they had to jump to it at two minutes' notice. I needed them to know how to react to an emergency as if it were as instinctive as scratching an itch; to know the difference between *Code Yellow* and *Code Red* like they knew the difference between their left and right bollock and exactly what to do in either situation. They'd been shown inside the Citadel, learning where everything was stored, so that the space was familiar and less frightening. I'd briefed them in detail on what might be happening up on the bridge at that point, the possible scenarios, the possible outcomes. As always, I did it as calmly as I could but you could often see the fear in their faces. Tricky not to cross that fine line between making them take it seriously and scaring the shit out of them. It was also important not to over-train them in case they became irritated and obstructive on the one hand or cocky and over-confident on the other. As a security man on a merchant ship, there were so many tightropes to walk.

With the captain's agreement, I supplemented our three-man team with crew members to act as lookouts on the bridge-wings and to be constantly checking the radar screen for those white dots. Above all, we put the vessel into 'lockdown' which meant that nobody could go out on deck unless the captain approved it for necessary maintenance or the operation of the ship. This 'house arrest' within the superstructure of the vessel wasn't easy for anyone, but it greatly lessened the risk of anyone being captured and held hostage in the event of an attack.

A big relief was that we had a fine captain. This time round, it was back to that rugged old Sean Connery type. Late 40s, from the Ukraine, Captain Dmitry was quite a guy. Like most men from that part of the world, he'd done national service; I reckon he could've stripped and reassembled an AK-47 even faster than I could. With Russians and Ukrainians I always sensed that they'd have no bother handling themselves in a real gun-fight and that they'd probably just love it if one came along.

In the evening after supper, Captain Dmitry liked to sit and tell stories of his time in the forces. He was a calm, cool bloke but with a good sense of humour. Just the sort you'd like on the bridge in time of trouble. If he wasn't telling stories, he was playing table tennis; I was pretty good but he was phenomenal, claiming to have been a state champion back home in Kiev. And if he wasn't playing table tennis, he was watching films. I lost count of how many times he asked if I had any on my computer.

Right from the start, the team had a good, easy relationship with Captain Dmitry. As a former military man, I reckon he respected us for our experience and our professionalism, though like us he thought it was nuts that we weren't armed. I also think he also knew that, on this trip, he really needed us. It was nice to be wanted for a change; to be welcomed and not seen as intruders to be tolerated.

So it was with a bit more confidence that I stood on the bridge-wing and watched the thin dark line of the Somali coast grow thicker and closer. Soon, the *Leviathan* sailed into its territorial waters and eventually, we could see the lights of Mogadishu twinkling in the distance.

'Well Jord, we're in Somalia,' said Buck Rogers as we stood on the bridge-wing.

'Yeah,' I replied quietly so nobody could hear. 'What the fuck are we doing here?'

Surprise, surprise, the port authority called to say our berth wasn't ready. A day or two, they reckoned. Bugger. Everyone on board wanted in and out of there as fast as possible. But when the two days were up, there was still no berth ready to take us. Then three days. The *Leviathan* anchored and floated gently in the 45C heat.

I doubled the watches: at least two guys at all times, six hours on, six hours off. Shorter shifts meant greater concentration on the potential dangers around you. It was a double-edged sword in that it messed up sleep patterns because the rest period was too short, but I felt that it was still the safest option. Focus was everything.

Every fishing boat anywhere near us had to be scrutinised and evaluated. At night, the ship had to be well-lit. This attracted the fish and so genuine fishermen always cast their nets close to the big merchant ships. By day, the 'bum-boats' came right up to the hull and it was almost impossible to swat them all away. There was always the fear that they were doing a recce of the ship for a later assault; fruit sellers by day, pirates by night. Hard times had led the Somalis to be serious multi-taskers.

In the early morning of the fourth day, I was asleep in my cabin. I'd just done the evening shift from 6pm to midnight. My phone rang.

'Get up here Jord,' said Buck from the bridge.

A small craft was behaving suspiciously, close to the anchor chain at the bow. This was totally different to the previous pirate approaches I've described. This time, there was no black radar screen on which two lonely dots would suddenly appear then advance upon us. The radar screen here was awash with dots from all the other vessels anchored nearby and from the smaller craft as well. It was like Piccadilly Circus on there, so it was next to useless for separating the good guys from the bad guys. The small boat in question had simply drifted closer to us. Nor had it been the usual skiff going like a bat out of hell; no gunshots, no rocket-propelled grenades across our bows. The *Leviathan* was stationary; there was no chance of running. In these crowded waters, it had just sidled up alongside and was now so close against the hull, we simply couldn't see what it was doing. We had no idea what we were up against.

I called Captain Dmitry to the bridge. As I'd expected, he was cool as the proverbial cucumber.

'I want to do something that's not in the rule-book,' I said. 'I want to go out and take a look.'

He looked me straight in the eye. By now, there was some trust between us.

'I thought we were in lockdown,' he replied.

'We are, but at the moment we're like blind men. I need to go outside.'

'Okay. Be careful.'

I asked Paul Riley to go with me. It was a risk for us both, but he immediately agreed. We were unarmed, remember. If this little craft *was* a pirate boat, if they were already scaling the hull, we were turning ourselves into potential hostages which would mean that no military force would try to rescue us. The concept of the Citadel could be undermined and this ship could be hijacked and held to ransom. For everyone on board, the next months of their life might be very different. And yet…

As Dad had said so often, I'd always be a soldier, first and last. It was pretty fucking tough to be a soldier without a gun. But, weapon or not, I still had my soldier's eyes and ears, my soldier's instinct and experience. In a situation like this, it seemed bonkers not to use them in the hope that they might win us some sort of advantage.

Leaving Captain Dmitry and Buck Rogers in control of the bridge, Paul and I went down the staircases inside the superstructure and crept out onto the deck. The *Leviathan* was about the length of three football pitches and we'd have to run the gauntlet of this vast open space; the only slight cover provided by the low roofs of the vast cargo holds and the small, onboard cranes which loaded and unloaded the dry goods onto the docks. In case the suspicious craft was in fact harmless, we carried a few rocket flares and a loud-hailer in order to shoo them away.

But a cautious peek over the side soon killed that notion. It was a skiff alright, up at the bow six or seven guys, armed with automatic rifles, starting to scale the hull. For a split second I asked myself if they could be coastguards or even the Somali navy. But that soldier's instinct kicked in. No way. These were pirates.

'Big trouble,' I hissed to Paul.

I radioed up to the bridge.

'Buck, ask the captain to trigger *Code Yellow*.'

It was high time to get out of there. Paul and I raced back along the length of the deck towards the tower of the super-structure, hoping that a bullet wasn't about to go whizzing past our ears. Yet again, it struck me that we were in the same plight as Rocky Mason had been on the Biscaglia; pirates almost on the deck and no guns to fight back with. I was buggered if I was jumping into these filthy, stinking, oil-stained waters. We made it to the superstructure, care-fully securing the external door behind us.

Back on the bridge, things had been racing too and they were now way ahead of us. From their higher vantage point, Buck and Captain Dmitry had been able to see that at least two pirates were now on board the ship. Having triggered *Code Yellow* as I'd asked, he and Buck had decided to go for *Code Red* about 30 seconds later. As team leader, this made me feel that I'd slightly lost control of the situa-tion by my decision to go out on deck, though I still didn't regret it. They'd also tried to radio the Somali port authori-ties but hadn't received a reply.

'There's something odd going on,' said Captain Dmitry. 'We've been in contact with these port guys every day since we dropped anchor. All very friendly. Now suddenly, they're not there. I wonder why?'

His question was ironic, said with a faint smile. We all knew the probable answer. Either the port people had some sympathy with the pirate 'cause' or were in active collusion with them. In their jolly phone calls with the *Leviathan*, had they managed to tease out some information about her security situation; like the fact that the guards weren't armed?

Unfortunately, the decision to trigger *Code Red* right on top of *Code Yellow* had caused some hysteria down below. Some of the crew had gone to the mustering point; others had fled straight to the Citadel. Despite my best efforts with the drills, I'd not foreseen that scenario. The calm, disciplined response I'd trained them to give had pretty much gone out of the porthole in the face of the real event. People were running around grabbing their personal possessions; something they'd been specifically instructed not to do.

'It's madness down there,' Paul Riley reported back to me on the bridge.

Captain Dmitry was shutting down and locking all the computers so the pirates couldn't gain access. But it was vital to switch one thing on. The Automatic Identification System (AIS), which told all nearby shipping, including the pirates, exactly where your ship was located, was always turned off when in Pirate Alley. But if an attack actually occurred, it was the only means by which the rescuers you prayed were on their way, would be able to pin you down. There were several occasions when, before rushing down to the Citadel, the crew had forgotten to do this and the rescuers couldn't bloody find them. A cock-up of major proportions. But you always had to make allowances for human error. We're all flesh and blood after all, especially in moments of enormous stress. There's an old military saying that 'no plan survives the first contact with the enemy'. The trick was to have a second plan ready in case the first one went pear-shaped.

But now it was time to abandon the bridge. And fast. Not an easy thing for the master of any vessel to do. The old cliché of the sea captain was that he disappeared under the waves, with a smart salute and his cap still on. Luckily, Captain Dmitry was a tough old bird, not the sentimental type at all.

The bridge of course was the pirates' destination; the heart and soul of the ship. But most of these huge vessels had been designed and built before the rise of Somali piracy. Their bridges hadn't been constructed to repel a serious armed attack. They were, in fact, alarmingly vulnerable; not unlike greenhouses, their windows made of glass tough enough to withstand a stormy sea but not the blast of an AK-47 or a rocket-propelled grenade. So there was precious little you could do to secure a bridge, apart from making its doorways as robust as possible with reinforcements of wood or metal bars and attaching the strongest locks you could find. Even if the attackers managed to blow them off, you might be able to slow them down. Anything to buy us a few more precious minutes and make sure that everyone gets to safety.

So hey, this was it. After all my uneventful transits, all the previous approaches, all those scary dots on the radar, even that grenade which had crashed into the side of the *Ocean Beauty*, I was finally heading into a Citadel. Not to stock it up, not as part of crew training, but to maybe save my life. Shit. This looked like being the big one.

CHAPTER 16

Into The Citadel

Every second counted now. Securing every door and gangway behind us, Captain Dmitry, Buck and I sped down to 'A' deck. This was the galley level, the mustering point under the *Code Yellow* procedure. By now, it should have been deserted, but there were still guys here who'd not responded to *Code Red*. With some of them, the language barrier meant communication wasn't that easy, especially when people were panicky and not always listening. But somehow we coped with gestures, shooing them like sheep further and further down into the bowels of the ship, still securing every door and staircase as we descended.

On the *Leviathan*, the Citadel had been created in the steering gear-room, one of the maze of smaller-rooms leading off the enormous engine hall. It was a reasonable space, about 15 metres long and reasonably wide. Naturally we'd chosen it by the usual criteria; that it had only one entrance which we could reinforce by the customary methods and which wasn't weakened by portholes or large ventilation shafts. Everything we needed had been installed. Food and water. Bedding and medical supplies. Torches and lamps in case the power supply was lost. But my mind raced as I looked quickly round the room again, trying to remember what was where, mentally ticking every box on my list.

Buck reminded me of one thing I'd forgotten.

'Boiler suits on, Jord,' he said.

The three of us slipped into the thin uniform which, if we were captured, would help us to blend in with the rest of the crew. Needless to say, security guards were less than popular with pirates; no point in making yourself a prime target for abuse.

Now the moment was here. Everyone had been accounted for. The door was closed and locked, the reinforcing metal bars slipped into place. That was it. We were in the Citadel. We had been forced to abandon the *Leviathan* to the men who had boarded her and were now trying to take control. I'd always imagined this moment of retreat as a kind of defeat, as the losing of a battle. But in this case it was unavoidable. We were unarmed. The ship was stationary in the anchorage and had no chance to run. The flaws in the basic protection measures had made them a feeble deterrent. Buck, Paul and I were just three guys after all; there was only so much we could do.

Once the door of the Citadel had been slammed and sealed, I looked around. There were about 25 of us. Apart from Captain Dmitry, Buck Rogers and a couple more, they were all men of about my age. A few, in the lower ranks, were little more than lads. And they were scared. There was no doubt about that.

Nobody said very much. Not that there was any need for silence. Even when a ship wasn't moving forward, the engine room and the surrounding area was still a noisy place. The power needed for electricity, ventilation, refrigeration, computer systems and half a dozen other reasons made sure there was a constant background racket. When working down here, the engineering crew wore ear defences. So in the Citadel, there was no need to whisper; the pirates were unlikely to hear us even if we'd decided to hold a karaoke session while we waited for rescue. That was the upside; the downside was that we couldn't hear the pirates either. We had no idea if they were still out on the decks, if they'd now penetrated the bridge or if they were hunting us down already and were right outside the door ready to blow the locks and hinges off with their guns or, heaven forbid, a grenade.

And this was my big problem. My first time locked in a Citadel and it had only taken about 10 minutes for me to realise that I couldn't bloody stand it. Not the claustrophobia thing; I'd once been the driver of a battle-tank after all. I just couldn't bear not knowing what was going on outside. Not knowing the reality of our situation.

I felt helpless, useless, impotent. Something had to be done. Obviously, it meant breaking the same rule I'd ignored earlier by going out onto the deck. The rule that prohibited you from making yourself a potential hostage, trashing the whole concept of the Citadel, not to mention any chance that the naval forces would attempt to storm the ship and rescue us.

'Okay, I'll come with you,' said Buck Rogers. 'I've got an idea.'

To Captain Dmitry and the crew, we explained why we wanted to go outside. We'd be gone for the shortest possible time. They didn't look happy, but they didn't try to stop us. We organised a password which would let us back into the safe-room. Paul would stay in charge of things while we were gone.

Buck and I opened the door an inch at a time. We had no idea if a row of Somali faces, armed with pistols and grenades, would be smiling at us on the other side. But it was clear. We ran quickly through the engine room, praying that we wouldn't fly around a corner and come face to face with the enemy. But it seemed that our layered defences on the levels above, all the locked doors and gangways, were still holding good. Buck led the way. From the direction we were heading, the penny soon dropped what his idea was.

The engine room gave access to the funnel of the ship. Rising up the inside of the funnel was a metal ladder used for maintenance.

'The vents?' I said.

'The vents,' he replied.

'Clever old fucker,' I said.

At various points up the height of the funnel were air vents, the topmost of which would provide a crystal clear view of the bridge. The ladder was at least 50 feet high. Not a job for the fainthearted, but I was game.

'No,' said Buck.' My idea, my call.'

He scampered up the ladder like a rat up a drainpipe. I stood below, my neck craned, my heart pumping. In just a couple of minutes, he was back down beside me.

'No sign of a soul,' he said. 'It's like the fucking *Mary Celeste*.'

If the attackers weren't there, where the hell were they? There was no obvious sign that the bridge had been broken into, but we couldn't be certain of that. Were they now heading downwards, deck by deck, getting closer to us all the time? It was far too dangerous to explore any further in order to find out.

Buck and I sprinted back to the Citadel, but we'd got back to safety with no more answers than we'd left with. It'd been a big risk for no reward.

But there was another problem to deal with and arguably far more important. Currently, we had no idea if any help was coming our way. When the crisis had started, the alarm system to the shipping company had been activated but things had moved so fast we just didn't know if any message had gone through. Nor had there been a chance to radio the UKMTO in Dubai, which was the major means of initiating any rescue attempt by the international naval forces. In other words, did anybody out there know we were in deep shit? There was only one way to find out. By trying to reach them again.

In line with best practice, all the relevant rescue phone numbers had been stored in the Citadel as well as on our sat-phones themselves. Captain Dmitry and I started ring-ing round. No joy. On call after call, the signal strength faltered then gave up the ghost. This shouldn't have hap-pened and I didn't know why. Maybe the antenna up on deck was faulty. Maybe there were so many other vessels in the vicinity that the channels were too crowded to cope. Damn and blast. Bloody technology. Miraculous when it works; crap when it doesn't. I saw the tension gather on the faces of the crew as they watched us fail and fail again to reach the outside world.

It was clear to me that to be certain the alarm really had been raised I needed to go back out of the Citadel for a second time, until I found a spot where the sodding sat-phone would work. And I now knew where that spot could well be. Up inside the funnel.

'Right, let's go,' said Buck.

'Nope, I'll go alone this time,' I replied.

'Don't be daft, Jord,' he said. 'You're the team leader. They need you here.'

I heard what he was saying but, somewhat to my shame, I wasn't listening. I could see that Captain Dmitry and the crew weren't happy either. I'd trained them well enough for them to know that, yet again, I was breaking the very rules I'd been so fierce about drumming into them. The chief officer, another Ukrainian, was especially blunt.

'By going outside, you're putting us all at risk,' he said. 'Isn't that the opposite of what you're here for?'

He was dead right of course. I tried to convince him that an attempt to summon help, trigger a rescue and hopefully save everyone from possible long-term captivity was worth making. But I had to admit it was a finely balanced judgment.

'Secure the Citadel behind me,' I said to Buck. 'I'll be back in no time.'

With my heart in my mouth, I inched open the fortified door and slipped out. The huge chamber of the engine-room was still empty. I stopped for a moment to see if I could hear anything whatever above the dull throb of the machinery. Like bullets blasting through the locks of the layered defences on the levels above. Even just shouting or running feet. But I heard nothing. The *Leviathan* seemed to be floating as peacefully on the calm water as she'd done for the past three days.

I reached the base of the funnel again and climbed up the ladder as fast as I could. Christ it was high; no way was

I going to look down. Luckily at the very top was a tiny platform, so I didn't have to hold the ladder in one hand and the sat-phone in the other, 50 feet above the floor. I was now perched at the highest point on the whole damn ship; to get any higher I'd have to be a frigging seagull. Through the vent in the funnel wall, there was still not a soul to be seen. Where were they?

I dialled the UKMTO number in Dubai. I made a mental note that if the signal didn't work at this height I'd sue the network one day. But hallelujah; it did. The problem was that the noise of the engine room far below me meant that I couldn't catch everything they were saying, but I knew they could hear me. So I gave them the ship's coordinates, outlined the situation and asked for assistance as soon as possible. But would it come? It was pot luck as to whether any resource was even remotely close to us or if we'd be sitting in the Citadel for days on end. But hey, at least my risk had worked. The outside world now knew we needed help pronto.

From my little eyrie, there was still nothing to be seen on the bridge. I also managed to cautiously open a tiny door in the funnel that looked down on the stern; but nobody was there either. Again, *where the fuck are they?* Were they already inside the superstructure, gradually burrowing down further and further in their search for us?

I raced back through the engine-room to the Citadel to give them the good news that the alarm had now definitely been raised and that, hopefully, help was on its way. At once, I saw that good news was badly needed.

It was now about six in the morning; not much more than an hour since the incident had started. The crew had been in the safe-room for no time at all, but I could already see the stress levels bubbling up like milk in a saucepan. Naturally, they'd all heard the stories of other pirate attacks which had gone pear-shaped and had led to violence against the captive seafarers. Young Filipino guys were crouched in corners, peeking at photographs of their nearest and dearest, wondering when, and maybe if, they'd see them again. Despite adequate ventilation, it was already hot in there after just an hour or so. I shuddered to think what it would be like in 12 hours' time or, God forbid, in two or three days. People were already knocking back our water supplies far too fast. I realised we'd underestimated. I asked them all to ration themselves or we'd soon be in difficulty. There had also already been a fair amount of nervous urinating. The yellow plastic buckets were no longer pristine.

To my surprise, I could see that even Captain Dmitry was stressed. No wonder though; it was probably harder for him than for any of us. Leaving his bridge and fleeing to the Citadel must have felt like abandoning his ship, that ultimate humiliation for the master of any vessel.

It'd be a fib to suggest that Buck, Paul and I weren't scared too, though the old professional reflexes had kicked in, which always carried you through. It'd be another fib to deny that there wasn't the surge of adrenalin that comes to every soldier when, after a long period of watching and waiting, he finally sees some action. Of course we had to be careful not to show that in front of those who we were trying to protect. I remembered Dad telling me the ethos of the Royal Marines: 'cheerfulness in the face of adversity.' But that could only go so far. Now, in the safe-room of the *Leviathan*, I had to gently tick off one of my guys for telling a joke and laughing. Never appropriate when there was fear in the air and in the eyes of the crew.

The three of us stood slightly apart, debating the situation and the worst case scenario. The big mystery was still exactly where the attackers were. We felt sure that, by now, they *must* have breached the bridge. Surely they must now be plunging deeper and deeper down into the hull, dismantling our layers of defence one by one, tracking down their quarry. By now they must have realised that we'd put the ship into lockdown and had gone into hiding. They'd also have twigged that the vessel had a security plan, that a rescue process had probably been triggered and that the clock was ticking against them. They had to find us fast.

No other scenario made sense. If they weren't doing that, why the hell had they bothered to board us in the first place, armed to the teeth? Just to nick a few laptops? Or to take selfies on the bridge to send to their adoring women? Some sort of testosterone 'high'?

With the limited equipment we'd had at our disposal, we'd done our utmost to reinforce the door to the Citadel, but we still worried about it. Until an assault actually took place, we couldn't be sure how well it would withstand determined firepower. We were especially concerned about an escape hatch that opened directly from the main deck of the ship into the engine-room. It was locked from the inside and there was a bloody great drop to the floor below but, if the pirates had rope ladders, it could well be our Achilles Heel.

Our best hope remained the chance that they'd never find the Citadel in the first place. The innards of these huge ships had literally dozens of internal doors, all looking pretty similar. Even if they did find the actual door, they had no way of knowing it was the right one unless they went to the bother of blowing it open. By this time, several hours might have passed since the beginning of the attack, during which the rescuers, assuming they were actually coming, would be getting ever closer.

'Jord, let me go out again,' said Buck.

'*What?* What for?'

'This is nuts, Jord,' he said. 'Where are they? What are they doing? Maybe they've ditched the attack.'

'Ok, go. Be careful.'

I secured the door behind him. In the safe-room, 25 faces stared at me. Captain Dmitry still grim, the chief officer still disapproving, most of the crew still scared.

We'd been in there less than two hours now, but the heat was pretty grim. The thought of even one day inside here was awful. People were ignoring my request to cut down on water. By now the three yellow plastic buckets were full with no means of emptying them. If I were ever in this situation again, I'd make sure there were a hundred buckets. A few had started pissing into the empty water bottles. Not nice.

I looked at my watch. Five minutes since Buck had gone. Ten. Fifteen. I tried to raise him by radio, but couldn't get a connection; the signal as crap as ever. Twenty minutes. I was seriously worried now. Had the attackers caught him? Did he now have a pistol at his head, as they demanded to know where the Citadel was? Had my gamble in letting him go outside gone spectacularly wrong? Would I find myself in a courtroom one day with the chief officer pointing a finger at me, saying it was all my fault?

Oh well, if I'd fucked up I might as well fuck up big time. I was going out to find Buck. By this point, Paul Riley was pretty unhappy with me too. Quite understandably, he didn't much want to be the last security man standing. Not quite what he'd envisaged on his very first job at sea.

'Please think what you're doing,' he said.

But I had. Outside the door of the Citadel again, I had no idea what I was going to find. But it was still deserted. The giant engines still throbbed and hummed. I ran to the bottom of the funnel and breathed a sigh of relief. There was Buck, at the top of the metal ladder, resting on the tiny platform, looking out through the vent.

There was too much engine noise to make myself heard, so I had to climb up underneath him.

'What's going on?' I said.

'They're on the bridge-wings' he replied. 'I can see three or four of them; a couple of them with AK-47s.'

'What about the others?' I asked. 'There were definitely six or seven in the skiff.'

'Fuck knows,' he replied. 'But I don't think they've even penetrated the bridge.'

Wow. That was the best news I could have heard. But we were far from being out of the woods yet. Anything could still happen. Was Buck right about the bridge? If he wasn't, where the hell were the other pirates? Would I suddenly look down from my perch on the ladder and see them grinning up at me with the barrel of a rifle pointing right up my arse?

'So what have they been doing all this time?'

'Selfies?' said Buck. 'Just poncing about?'

I used the opportunity to make another call to

UKMTO, to try and find out if any help was on its way. But this time, even this high up, the damn signal wouldn't work. But Buck and I were slightly more confident now. We stayed there for half an hour or more, taking turns to keep watch through the vent in the funnel and making swift trips back to the Citadel to keep the captain informed of what was happening. Suddenly, Buck gestured to me to come back up the ladder.

'They've left the bridge-wing,' he said, 'and in a hurry.'

'Where are they now?'

'Dunno,' he replied. 'No, hang on. I can see them again. They've moving up towards the bow.'

Because of the engine-room noise, we didn't hear it at first. The cavalry. But soon, Buck could see it.

'It's a chopper!' he said. 'It's circling right above us.'

Hallelujah.

'They're on the run. They're scrambling over the side back to their boat.'

I couldn't believe our luck. The chances of Combined Task Force 151 having a helicopter patrol in the vicinity had been so slim. But they'd got here in not much more than an hour. As good as the bloody RAC. Awesome.

I tried to contact the UKMTO on the sat-phone but again the signal strength wasn't good enough. But it didn't matter. All we'd really needed was something to scare off the pirates. The helicopter had appeared out of the skies like an avenging angel and done just that. It circled above the *Leviathan* for quarter of an hour, then wheeled away. Job done. I'd certainly be sending a Christmas card to UKMTO. Maybe even a Valentine.

Buck and I went back to the Citadel. We'd been gone for

at least 45 minutes. The faces inside seemed even grimmer, the heat even worse. Caution was still the watchword but I allowed myself a quick smile of reassurance. It was great to see some of the fear leave people's eyes and some hope now takes its place.

We updated them on what had just happened, but emphasised that everyone must stay where they were for the time being.

'You can't guarantee that every pirate has left my ship?' asked Captain Dmitry.

'No sir,' I replied. 'We were never sure precisely how many had boarded. And we're not yet certain if every single one of them has now gone.'

'So we need to find that out?' he asked.

'Yes sir. Till then, the Citadel stays functional.'

'Okay, but this time I'm coming with you.'

'Sir, I'd feel much happier if you stayed safe here for the time being.'

But Captain Dmitry now reasserted his authority over me and I wasn't going to challenge it.

The three of us eased ourselves out of the Citadel, the metal bars sliding back into place behind us. With maximum caution, like cats walking on a hot tin roof, we progressed upwards, level by level, unlocking the fortified doorways and the grilles over the staircases, then securing them behind us. Everything seemed to be just as it had been at the moment we'd all fled downwards. No signs of attempted break-in.

With every door we unlocked, we prepared to face the possibility of coming face to face with a pirate; one of those we'd not counted in and not counted out. If it were just one guy, could the three of us conceivably take him on? Even though we were unarmed, the power of Buck Rogers, built like a tank and half-covered with tatts, plus the tough, military-trained Captain Dmitry might just do the job.

Finally we reached the last door, the one that led up from the interior onto the bridge. Here too, thank Christ, our fortifications had held. Still, we opened it gingerly, ready to slam it again, lock it and run like hell back towards the Citadel. But the bridge was empty, quiet as a church apart from the distant hum of the engines. It was about eight in the morning now; the sun was streaming in through the big wide windows as the *Leviathan* bobbed gently on the water. It felt good to be back in the light again; like miners coming up from the pit.

Now, finally, we saw the only physical evidence of what had happened in the past few hours. The external doors to the bridge had been attacked with considerable force but, miraculously, had held. Their gunfire had easily blown the locks but our reinforcing measures had defeated them.

What had they done next? We'd never know exactly; it could only be guesswork. We'd glimpsed a mini armoury in their skiff earlier, but maybe they'd been too nervous to use their weaponry in the close confines of the bridge-wing. Maybe they'd farted around, not knowing what to do, bickering among themselves. And then the helicopter had come. The last straw. They'd turned and fled.

'We've been lucky,' I said to Captain Dmitry. 'It could easily have been very different.'

But it had been amateur night. If it had been a professional production, carefully planned and well-funded, they'd have had the equipment to break into the bridge and the Citadel too, if they'd managed to locate it. Instead of standing here on a sunny morning, awash with relief, contemplating just one damaged doorway, the pirates could have been in control. A pistol would have been at Captain Dmitry's temple as they forced him to start the engine and turn the *Leviathan* northwards towards one of the pirate-ports further up the coast.

Once the ship had been moored off the pirate village, the guys who'd done the actual hijacking would have found themselves sidelined. The criminal organisation would have taken over. From the shore, a new squad of pirates would be ferried out to guard the hostages on a shift pattern. Cooks would be imported to feed the pirates and the crew, however grim the latter's provisions might be. The pirates' negotiator would arrive on board, evaluating the worth of the ship and its cargo, working out an acceptable ransom figure then adding a few more million dollars just for fun. In the distant offices of the shipping companies, the usual process would have kicked in. Waiting for the ransom demand. Bringing in their own negotiators. Dealing with the frightened families of the crew. Who knows how long it would all have taken? The average time before a hijacked crew was released was about five to six months, but nobody could forget those poor guys who'd been held captive for several years.

But, as I'd said to Captain Dmitry, we'd been lucky. So very, very lucky,

Buck and I went out on the decks to double-check there were no intruders left, hiding somewhere in a quiet corner, ready to pounce. But it was clear.

All round us, the day was beginning and the anchorage

had woken up. The usual crowd of fishing-boats and 'bum-boats' had started to appear, streaking across the water. Most were skiffs with several men in them. It was that old problem. There was no way it was possible to tell which were innocent and which might be sizing you up for an attack later. Maybe one of them was even the skiff which had just boarded us. It wasn't unknown for the same ship to be attacked more than once, even within 24 hours. The pirates, angered by their failure the first time, would come back for a second go; this time better equipped and with a clear idea of the layout of the ship and its security measures. So it wasn't paranoia to see every little skiff as a major threat.

'This place is a bloody nightmare, Jord,' said Buck, looking out over the sea. 'There's no way we can keep this ship safe here.'

He was right. We'd sailed into the lion's den and, for the past three days, had been sitting here inviting it to bite us. Well, now it just had and we'd survived this time. Next time, we might not.

I contacted UKMTO in Dubai to let them know the threat had receded. And to thank them too. It turned out that the helicopter had been sent from an American warship that had just happened to be in the area. Not for the first time in history, we Brits had been saved by the Yanks.

On the bridge, Captain Dmitry had put in his usual morning call to the port authorities about the current status of our berth on the dockside. He didn't mention that the *Leviathan* had just been illegally boarded. As usual, they were helpful and friendly. But where had they been when we'd needed them earlier? Like the fish wriggling in the bottom of the skiffs, something stank a little.

We released the crew from the Citadel and de-briefed them on exactly what had happened. Some of them were clearly shaken up, though trying hard not to show it. During the years of Somali piracy, it wasn't just those seafarers who were held in long-term captivity who were traumatised by their experiences. For some, from the captain to the lowliest member of the crew, an illegal boarding like ours today, or even just a suspicious approach, could be a deeply disturbing event which made them abandon their life in the merchant navy. Especially those who'd had to retreat inside a Citadel and felt their futures shrink down into this hot, noisy, uncomfortable prison from which, they imagined, they might never be set free.

One young officer cadet would soon go to Captain Dmitry and ask to leave the ship when we reached Mombasa so he could fly home to the Philippines, though eventually he decided to stay the course. But don't let anyone imagine that seafarers could shake off these attacks like a dose of the flu and go right back to playing table tennis and watching films. The pirates of Somalia, whether they triumphed or not, always left their mark.

Once again, these events instantly changed seafarers' attitudes to the tedious restrictions of security. The crew became a hundred times more alert and watchful and nobody complained any more about the interruptions my security drills caused to their normal duties.

In the anchorage off Mogadishu, the rest of the day was much like any other as the *Leviathan* went on waiting for her slot on the dockside to come up. But how long was that going to take? One more day, one more week, still sitting in the lion's den?

'Sir, let's get out of here,' I said to Captain Dmitry later that day. He agreed.

The *Leviathan* started her great engines, turned her prow away from Somalia and sailed 10 miles further out to sea. Not far enough in my book, but better than nothing. We increased our look-outs and sat there for another two days till our great chums at the port authority finally deigned to let us come into the dockside. Once we tied up, we were in and out of there within 24 hours. I imposed the tightest possible access control on the gangways. Even a mosquito couldn't have got past me without the correct ID. Nobody, whether crew or security, was allowed off the ship. There would be no interesting tourist excursions into downtown Mogadishu or brief encounters with the local lovelies. No postcards would be going home saying 'Greetings from Somalia'. What a sad country it must be, where people would try to hijack a ship that was carrying desperately needed aid for its own population. But I didn't feel angry, just sad for them all, even the pirates. I counted the minutes till we eased away from the pirate kingdom and headed south towards Mombasa.

What had happened to the *Leviathan* was a rare event. Very few ships with a security team aboard, whether armed or unarmed, were successfully boarded by pirates; the presence of the team usually being a sufficient deterrent. But maybe this gang of pirates hadn't even bothered with a recce and simply didn't know we were there. It really was amateur night. And that was what probably saved us.

The news of the assault on *Leviathan* soon got around the private marine security industry. My employers at the time were strangely delighted. Over the next six weeks, my CEO took me to meetings in London, New York, Singapore and Athens where I'd tell the story to the boards of various shipping companies. Jordan Wylie, proud leader of the heroic team who had sent the pirates packing, became an asset to be advertised. Naturally I was well aware I was being used to pull in new business, but I didn't mind. Many private maritime guards, no matter how many transits they did, ever experienced so much as a suspicious approach let alone an assault or an actual boarding. But I'd seen 'action'. It seemed as if I wore invisible medals.

Though not of course in the eyes of everyone. I doubt if the chief engineer had been the only crew member who'd been deeply unhappy about Buck Rogers and I going outside the Citadel; not just once but several times. In their view, I'd broken all my own rules and compromised everyone's safety. I totally understood that point of view but in the same scenario I'd probably do it again. Whether in the military or in security operations in hostile environments, you literally live or die by your decisions. On land or sea, it's about making tough choices in stressful circumstances. You rely on your experience, your expertise, your colleagues and, perhaps above all, on that soldier's instinct to help you make the right one.

I've said before that guys like Buck Rogers, Rocky Mason, Macca McFarland and me would always be soldiers first and last. It wouldn't matter what other jobs we might do in the future: in certain scenarios, that soldier inside us would always come out like a rash. And I think that was what happened with me that morning on the *Leviathan*. My military instinct told me that I needed to know what was happening outside the Citadel in order to properly protect those frightened people inside it. It was a sort of built-in barometer that helped you to assess risk, to act on a hunch and to have a sixth sense for when there was real danger – or indeed the lack of it. For men like us, danger was something you could smell in the wind. We'd learnt to do that in places like Iraq, Afghanistan and Libya. In short, on the *Leviathan* I'd let the soldier in me conquer the security team leader. And I can't really pretend to be sorry for that. If I hadn't, the cavalry might never have rescued us.

We reached Mombasa safely, where everyone was allowed to let their hair down, except for Buck who didn't have any. Then we turned northwards towards Karachi and finally back to Oman. The rest of the voyage was uneventful, thank God, though I kept security tight as a coiled spring.

Apart from that, the life of the ship drifted back to something like normality. Though perhaps not entirely. I sensed a longing among the crew, far greater than usual, to reach the end of the voyage and head for home. I wondered how many would have tearful discussions with their loved ones about going back to sea; though for many there would be little choice. For Paul Riley, the third man on my team, this trip would be his first and last as a maritime security guard. He eventually settled in Dubai, got married and started a career as an insurance salesman. I guess there's a lot to be said for that. But for the time being, we sailed back towards Oman through placid seas. Every evening, I played table tennis with Captain Dmitry and was slaughtered every time. Life went on.

On the evening after the pirates had boarded us, I'd

gone down to the Citadel with Buck to re-stock it with supplies in case there was a second incident. The first thing we saw were the three yellow plastic buckets, full up to the brim, and the various water bottles which now contained rather different fluids than their original contents.

'I'm not emptying those,' said Buck.

'Well I'm not bloody doing it,' I replied.

'Toss you for it.'

'Okay.'

'Here we go then.'

'Oh bollocks,' I said.

CHAPTER 17

End of the Gold Rush

In 2011, the same year that the *Leviathan* was boarded, the pirates of Somalia were having their *annus mirabilis*. In the scruffy, windswept villages of Eyl and Harardhere, in the ports of Bossasso in the north and Kismayo in the south, all along that endless, barren coastline on both sides of the Horn of Africa, they were making whoopee in a big way. The loot seemed to be rolling in faster than the waves broke onto the beaches. Pirates zoomed round in their brand new SUVs, girls clinging to their arms, flashing wads of notes and getting hyper on the *khat* leaves they chewed from dawn till dusk.

It was in 2011 that the phenomenon of Somali piracy reached its peak. A total of 237 ships were attacked, 28 of them successfully hijacked with an estimated cost of around $7 billion. Not bad for what had started as a bunch of grumpy fishermen wanting to be Robin Hood.

It's my opinion, surprise surprise, that it was the increasing presence of private security guards that provided the breakthrough resource which finally out-ran the pirates. The simple, irrefutable fact is that not one single merchant ship which carried private armed security guards was ever successfully hijacked and held to ransom.

When the tide finally turned against the brigands, it

turned with unbelievable speed. In 2012, just one year after the *annus mirabilis*, the number of attacks dropped like a stone to just over 30 and successful hijacks plummeted to only seven. It's hard to account for the suddenness of the fall but, apart from vessels now being harder to hijack, an increasing number of pirates were now being captured by the international navies, not to mention the tragic estimate that as many as half of all Somali pirates may well have drowned on the job.

For guys like me, there was a spectacular irony to all this. As Somali piracy appeared to be fading away like a bad smell on the breeze, we became the victims of our own success. In the boardroom of some huge shipping company in Copenhagen, I'd imagine the conversation probably went something like this…

'Well, excellent news Hans. No reported attacks for three months now.'

'Yes but let's not count our chickens just yet Christian.'

'No no, of course not. But maybe we could look at trimming our costs just a little.'

'In what way Christian?'

'Well, I was just looking at our expenditure on the security teams. It's pretty eye-watering don't you think?'

'Yes it certainly is. But it seems to have been the security guards who've knocked this damn thing on the head, wouldn't you say?'

'I wouldn't argue with that Hans. They're all excellent chaps, every last man of them. Credit where it's due and all that.'

'Absolutely. I understand that a lot of them came from my own old regiment. And you won't find better men anywhere.'

'Well, that's my point in a way. We've been paying for the very best military men to protect our ships. But now, if this issue seems to be drifting away, might we not do just as well with slightly less expensive people?'

'Wouldn't that be a tad risky Christian?'

'Not necessarily. The British teams have been training up the crews in security for ages now. Teaching them to protect themselves, as it were. I really do think the situation has changed quite substantially, wouldn't you agree?'

'You may well be right Christian. After all, I suppose it all just boils down to a chap on the deck waving a gun and looking fierce. Not exactly brain surgery is it?'

'Quite. And at the moment we're paying out a small fortune.'

'Yes and we have the shareholders to think of, after all.'

'As it happens Hans, I've just been given the name of a security company working out of Mumbai. Their chaps might not be quite top-drawer, but their rates are surprisingly reasonable. I rather thought I might send them an email. What do you think?'

'Fine Christian. Why not? No harm in that.'

I reckon it was a hundred little chats like that which brought an end to the Gold Rush. Although the hefty sums paid to security teams were fairly small beer compared to the other costs of running a merchant fleet, they were still substantial for enterprises trying to cope with a worldwide recession post-2008. Like any housewife in Sainsbury's, deciding to go for a cheaper side of beef than she normally bought, shipping companies tried to make cuts wherever they could. Did it really matter if the beef wasn't quite so delicious? Did it really matter if the security team came from Mumbai instead of Poole?

It didn't happen overnight of course, but by 2012 my bank manager back home might have noticed that the wonga rolling into my account wasn't quite as impressive as it had been. And the same thing was happening to hundreds, maybe thousands, of British ex-military men who'd dashed so eagerly to Heathrow and onto those planes heading for the seas around the Horn of Africa. At the beginning of the Gold Rush in 2008, there had been only about five private maritime security companies, all of them British. By 2012, there were at least 100; all of them competing in an overcrowded marketplace and already reducing their rates of pay in order to undercut the competition. The main ways to save money were manpower and logistics support. In other words, it was bye-bye to the five-star hotels. In the places where we found ourselves nowadays, we'd be less likely to see Daniel Craig by the pool than Bert and Doris Scroggins from Scunthorpe. The days of wine and roses were definitely over.

So when, on top of all that, the perceived need for our services began to diminish, it was double whammy. The boys in the back bedrooms with the laptops began to move on to pastures new. Even the bigger security companies started to amalgamate or to look quickly for other sources of revenue. But it would be the guys on the ships who took the biggest hit. Like any Gold Rush of previous centuries, this one had been a gamble. For a few years it had paid off spectacularly, but not anymore.

Sometimes, it wasn't just a question of losing income. If the company you worked for suddenly went under, you might find yourself marooned in dangerous waters with no means of getting home. In 2014, a large maritime security firm would go phut, leaving about a hundred of their guys stranded on various tankers and container ships all over Pirate Alley, and reportedly owing a sum in unpaid salaries and supplier invoices that ran into the millions. Some of those waiting ashore for their next transit would find themselves homeless when the company villas were repossessed.

At the risk of sounding like a smart git, I'd seen this coming and I'd laid my plans. In a wider world context, the issue of Somali piracy was becoming, so to speak, a drop in the ocean. Security issues, not just maritime, were now at the top of the agenda for governments and corporations around the globe. Yet often the levels of training were haphazard at best and woeful at worst.

I'd observed this so clearly in the early days of the Gold Rush when everything was largely unregulated. The days when we'd not had decent weaponry, enough ammo or protective clothing. When we'd found ourselves on vessels whose ways and cultures we hadn't understood. The times we'd had to improvise, ludicrously, in the face of danger by creating Dick the Dummy and his band of brothers. It'd all been a bit like the Wild West. Only slowly had a degree of governance and discipline crept in. And it was here that I'd seen the window into my future. Suppose all these deficiencies that had driven me nuts for so long were the key to my own way forward?

When the *Leviathan* had reached the relative safety of Mombasa, I'd been on watch one evening, staring out from the bridge-wing across the harbour. Once again, these long empty hours were the perfect time to think hard about how well my life was going – or not. Suddenly an idea crashed into my brain.

If all these people needed training, why didn't I do it? By now I had as much practical experience as anyone and I'd just started studying for my BA Hons, which would give me a much broader understanding of the complex issues involved as well as a lot more credibility. If anyone could devise an effective training programme for security professionals, surely it was me? In the cool light of morning, the idea was still there and growing in my mind. How could I set the proverbial ball rolling? And I could hardly do it all by myself.

On a hunch I managed to contact an old mate from the army called Sean O'Keefe. Sean was a Blackpool boy like me. He'd had quite a tough start in life, growing up in foster care and getting into trouble. Like so many others, he'd found his direction in the armed forces where he made his mark in many ways, especially in Iraq and Afghanistan where he'd worked with the US special forces as a covert surveillance specialist. After leaving the army, he'd gone back to Iraq and for seven years had worked very successfully in private security in the highly difficult post-war period. Though our career paths had never crossed since our army days, we'd somehow stayed in touch. In some ways, we were two peas in a pod. Both lads whose military careers had opened up new horizons and opportunities; both of us wanting to provide our children with some of the things we'd never had.

Now, as luck would have it, Sean wanted to be much more at home with his two children. He was intrigued by

my idea and in no time we'd worked out a plan. He would
begin to set up the company in the UK, create a website
and find premises while, in the short term, I'd stay on the
ships, building up valuable contacts in the shipping industry and developing the training programme in detail. At
this point, the piracy bubble hadn't quite burst yet and
there was still potential in the market. Each of us bunged
£1,500 into the pot and, in spring 2011, when Pirate Alley
was busier than ever, off we went.

The Training Wing, our security training and education
enterprise, was a great success. We based it first at Tidworth
in Wiltshire, one of the biggest military garrisons in the
UK. Next we opened up in Liverpool, where there was
more maritime business. Soon we were employing a large
number of staff and, within a year, it had become the go-to
place for instruction in maritime security. Our client-base
was twofold: firstly, guys like us who still wanted to leave
the military to go into private security; secondly, security
companies and shipping companies themselves who had
come to realise the commercial advantage of offering really
well-trained staff who would contribute to the risk reduc-
tion of anyone who employed them.

As we proved our worth, the graduates of our courses
were awarded accreditations from bodies such as the gov-
ernment-run Maritime and Coastguard Agency, the
Department for Transport and City and Guilds. Our big
USP was that we always worked hard to place them in jobs
at the end of their course. Within a couple of years, we'd
trained around 3,500 security personnel. We even won an
award from the Chamber of Commerce as *Best Business Of
The Year*. Me a businessman? Who'd have thought it?

CITADEL

Certainly not Mrs Fennell, my old teacher. I resisted the temptation to send her a copy of the citation.

Of course the irony was that now we were turning out all these well-trained people to work in maritime security, the Gold Rush was in its decline. Increasingly, the Brits were drifting out of it and being replaced by men from the less-developed countries, especially the Indian subcontinent and it wasn't long before we started running courses there. However, people smuggling, weapons smuggling and the rising threat of cyber attack were the game-changers. Graduates of our training programmes weren't likely to be out of work for long.

At first though, I hedged my own bets, keeping one foot on the ships and the other on *terra firma*. For a while, I continued working in London for a major player in the French and Italian security markets. I owe a lot to my bosses there, who mentored me and provided exactly the chances I needed to expand my skill-set. As their operations manager I was in charge of sending teams out to the ships but much of this was land-based, which reflected the new priorities in the industry. I helped organise combat medical courses for the French Foreign Legion in Provence. I was sent out to win new business, develop projects and liaise with governments in Iraq, Afghanistan, Nigeria, Libya and the United Arab Emirates. My new 'mates' were diplomats and politicians. It was heady stuff. A long way from standing on a bridge-wing with a pair of binos, scratching my arse.

I also spent a year as ops manager in Djibouti, the small state immediately next to Somalia, but a very far cry from that sad place. Djibouti's strategic position and enviable political stability meant that it has always been a perfect base for PMSCs as well as many other Western companies with interests in the Middle East and Africa. It was also the location of the largest American military installation on the continent. The Djibouti authorities had always been a big support to international shipping during the prime years of Somali piracy. For a predominantly Muslim country, it was pretty relaxed; no problems about going for a beer in a bar. I enjoyed myself there, but I always had to remember that I was a white man in an alien culture and needed my wits about me at all times. I liked the simplicity of life in Djibouti. It reminded me that the five-star hotels and the flash life I'd got a bit used to in recent years were all very nice but not really necessary for happiness and fulfilment.

I even did some close-protection work, including a riotous stint as security manager for the Italian football team and members of the sports media during the European Championships. That was a laugh. Mario Balotelli, the Italian striker was a crazy, wonderful guy. I once answered my bedroom door to be hit in the face by a jet from Mario's water-pistol. It seemed to be my lot in life to be surrounded by the wild boys.

On top of all this, I was also exploring opportunities in West Africa and the Gulf of Guinea where sadly another strain of piracy was emerging. But I knew it was daft to keep on riding so many horses, so I took the leap of faith and decided that I would finally say goodbye to working on the ships. From early 2010 till mid-2012, I'd notched up nearly 120 transits. Not bad. And I'd survived it. I was sad to leave the company after all they'd done for me, but the Training Wing was now going such great guns that Sean O'Keefe deserved a lot more of my time. He needed me hands-on.

But there was more to it than that. Like Sean, I knew I just had to spend more time with my nearest and dearest. Working in London, I was at least getting home to Laura and Evie much more often, but those brownie points had been cancelled out by my spell in Djibouti. Gradually, I'd realised I was becoming a stranger to my little girl. It was her mother she ran to and listened to, not me. Who could blame her? Who did this guy think he was, coming into their home and telling her what to do? I knew that, if I wasn't careful, our relationship might be permanently damaged. But it was the sudden end of another precious relationship that really brought home to me the price I was paying for my life away from home.

In May 2012, on what turned out to be my very last transit, I was standing on the bridge of a ship when somebody passed me a note. But I was on duty, so I stuffed the note in my pocket to read later. An incident had just taken place. We were sailing through the Bab el Mandeb Strait at the mouth of the Red Sea when we'd had a suspicious approach. We couldn't see their weapons but had spotted their ladders. Few genuine fishermen carried 15 feet ladders so they definitely weren't looking for that night's dinner. We fired a few warning shots and they'd fled, but there was a tense atmosphere on board and everyone's nerves had been badly jangled. When I finally remembered to read the note, it was like a punch in the guts.

It said that a message had been received to inform me that my grandmother had died suddenly in Blackpool. Nana and I had been incredibly close all my life; as a boy, I'd spent nearly as much time in her house as I had in my

own. In every way she'd been a second mother; her love
and her guidance always there for me, no matter what. She
was an amazing lady, one of a kind. Losing her was like
losing a piece of myself. The note also said that I would be
allowed to use the satellite phone to call home, but added
that the cost would be added to my end-of-mission invoice
for petty expenses while on board. Bastards.

When I finally got through, poor Mum was in a right old
state. Nana had passed away without any warning, but how
I wished I'd been in the UK and perhaps had the chance to
say goodbye to her or at least to try and comfort Mum. But
here I was, stuck on a ship, thousands of miles away. It
taught me two things. Firstly, that you never know when
you're saying goodbye for the last time, so make sure the
person always knows how you feel about them. Secondly,
that it was time for Jordan Wylie to go home.

In Blackpool, they held back the funeral till I could get
there. Carrying Nana to her rest was one of the toughest
things I'd ever had to do. All the memories came flooding
back. The story of the time she'd left me in my pram in the
corner shop, only remembering when she'd got home and
sat down with a cuppa, then racing in a panic all the way
back again to find me still safe beside the frozen foods.

Another member of my wider family, a guy about my
age, could only moan about how much of his day the
funeral service was taking up. Nana had been good to
him all his life, far more than he'd deserved and now he
begrudged the time to say goodbye to her. He'd rather
have been down the pub with his mates. If I'd ever really
wanted to belt someone, it was at that moment. But Nana
wouldn't have wanted that. Just like Mum and Dad, she'd

shown me that there was a better way to live your life. It didn't matter a damn if you'd not been born with a silver spoon in your mouth. You aimed for the highest standards, and even if you sometimes fell short, at least you were heading in the right direction. If you kept on trying, you'd get there in the end.

Nana's life was over but, if I was lucky, most of mine was still to come. I was only 30 now. The pirates of Somalia hadn't got me. Hopefully I still had plenty of time to make her proud.

So when I flew out of Jeddah back towards Britain for my grandmother's funeral, I tried to look forward and not back. But it was impossible not to remember that, for one group of people, the welcome dip in Somali piracy had strictly limited impact. The seafarers of the merchant ships who were still being held as hostages all around the Horn of Africa.

At this point, the crew of the cargo ship *Iceberg-1*, captured in 2010 off the coast of Yemen and more or less abandoned by its owners, was still six months away from freedom. The hijack of the Taiwanese fishing-trawler *Naham 3* off the Seychelles in March 2012 would last even longer. It would be over four years before those captives were released, in late 2016, telling tales of abuse and torture easily equal to those suffered by the men on the *Iceberg-1*. A year-and-a-half after the actual hijacking, the battered *Naham 3* had sunk at its moorings off the coast of Somalia and the crew transferred to a camp in a forest, treated like animals and forced to eat rats to survive. The captain had been shot dead on the day of the attack and two other crewmen had died of disease during their captivity; their bodies bundled into a freezer. The *Naham 3* incident served to remind the world yet again just how vicious and barbaric the Somali pirates could be, especially if things didn't go the way they'd planned.

I've already talked about the 'excuses' for Somali piracy: the illegal fishing and the destruction of their fishing-grounds; the disgraceful dumping of toxic waste, believed to have killed or maimed many thousands of Somalis. All of that is true and indisputable, so it was a sad thing that this then morphed into a massive criminal enterprise which sucked in and corrupted so many young men. Nothing can forgive the killing, torture and dreadful abuse carried out by some pirates against their fellow human beings.

But however much I wanted to defeat the pirates of Somalia, however hard I was willing to fight against them, I'd be lying if I pretended not to see some parallels between their lives and my own. Like them, I'd come from a place where people often had to struggle to survive. Like them, I wasn't expected to make much of a mark in life. Okay, the horrors suffered by the people of Somalia make the problems faced by the working-class of Blackpool seem like a walk in the park, but the basic scenario maybe isn't that different. In Somalia today, there is widespread famine; in Blackpool today, there are food banks and the town remains one of the UK's most deprived places with stratospheric rates of teenage pregnancy and illegal drug use. So maybe it's just a matter of degree. Maybe the effect on human beings is pretty much the same. A sense of utter hopelessness about the future.

I know how easy it would have been for me to have gone badly off the rails; I'd seen that all too clearly among guys

I'd grown up with, not to mention among members of my own extended family. Nor had I ever forgotten the time I'd gobbed off at the policeman in the park and ended up cooling off in a cell. I'd been rescued by the example of my amazing parents and my unique grandmother who together had given me the moral compass I'd needed to move myself onto a better path.

But if I'd been born in Somalia instead of Lancashire, what might have happened to me? I wonder how many Somali mums and dads, as decent and caring as my own, had watched sadly as their kids had turned to piracy and other criminal activities while the country disintegrated around them? How many dreams of something better had been ground down into the dusty, rubble-strewn streets of Somalia's towns and villages, devastated by a quarter-century of civil war? No wonder the temptation of a wad of money larger than you'd ever imagined was so irresistible. Buy that flashy SUV to swan around and show off in. Pull the prettiest girl in the village and give her anything she wants. Instead of being a sad no-hoper, you'd be a big man – at least till the money ran out. There was precious little difference between what motivated the young pirates of Somalia and the lads from the backstreets of Blackpool. The yearning for something better. Who was I to judge them too harshly?

As I'd flown away from the Middle East after that very last transit, I had ended a chapter that had changed me forever. At least I had that priceless asset, hope for the future. I'd learned enough about life by now to be convinced that, if I worked hard enough, my dreams stood a good chance of coming true. Few Somalis could say the same. So

CHAPTER 18

New Horizons

One dark night years ago, when I was still a raw recruit in the army, I'd found myself sitting on a wet, miserable Salisbury Plain during some exercise or other. Beside me was my troop leader. He wasn't much older than me but was, needless to say, a hell of a lot better-spoken and educated. Neither of us was exactly having fun.

'So what are you going to do if you ever leave the army sir?' I asked, for want of something better to say.

He looked at me with a wistful smile.

'I'm going to be a racehorse trainer, Trooper Wylie,' he replied. 'I'm going to have my own stable and breed only winners.'

His name was Jamie Snowden and eventually he did just that. Today he's a very successful trainer with many triumphs under his belt, including a Cheltenham Festival winner.

I'm sure he asked me the same question in return but I don't remember now what I answered. No doubt I mumbled something vague and woolly, because I really had no idea. Anyway, back then the peak of my ambition was to be a regimental sergeant-major, which was about as high as any NCO was ever going to get.

But when, in 2012, I finally gave up fighting the pirates of Somalia and returned to the UK, I had a pretty clear idea of where I was heading. In some ways, I was the same boy from Blackpool that I'd ever been, but in other ways I wasn't. I'd seen so much more of life now and lived on a far wider canvas. I'd mixed with people from many different countries and cultures, all of which had left a mark that couldn't be erased, nor did I want it to be. But those changes in me were going to come at a price a bit further down the road.

My business interests and investments went from strength to strength and I realised I had transitioned into a fully-fledged entrepreneur. I soon discovered that, in commerce, absolutely everything was about cost; outgoings versus profit. In the army for instance, you could fire as many rounds of ammo as you wanted and nobody's going to invoice you at the end of the month. But in the private sector, everything has to be accounted for. In many ways, it's a far tougher gig. An old army friend used to say that 'you can't hide in the jungle'; the apparent paradox meaning that you're actually very exposed and need all your senses to be alert to hidden dangers. If you can't survive, you'll be 'found out'. That described the commercial world to a tee. Unlike in the forces, you needed to be a hell of a lot more than just a 'time-server'. You sure wouldn't last long if you were. The bottom line was the bottom line.

But the upside of that was being master of your own destiny. You're never ever that in the forces. It's truly awful to see people being killed in Iraq and there's nothing you can do about it. But in business, though the pressures may be intense, finding a solution is nearly always possible if you're prepared to give it your best shot. So in that sense it's far more rewarding; a truer reflection of your own personal abilities. So I won't mind too much if my gravestone reads, 'Here lies Jordan Wylie. He gave it his best shot.'

One day, an old mentor named Gilles Capelle got in touch. He was now working with a large, French-based company called Sovereign Global, which was delivering training programmes for the United Nations in Africa. The UN had asked for some British training expertise and Gilles had recommended me. Then in 2013, Sovereign Global, which worked across many areas of the security industry as one of the world's largest providers of training, mentoring and logistics support, offered to take over the Training Wing. Yikes. Sean and I were tremendously proud of what we'd achieved and it wasn't easy to hand over our 'baby', but we'd learnt that there's no sentiment in business and it made commercial sense.

I was part of Sovereign Global's takeover too and so became an employee of this very sizeable concern. These days, rather than training up individuals, the Training Wing more often works for organisations and even governments of the less developed countries, teaching them the techniques and practices that can help them to help themselves. It's worthwhile, satisfying work and I love doing it.

In 2015, I became the CEO of Sovereign's UK operations. In my craziest dreams, I'd never have imagined myself in a sharp suit, collar and tie, sitting at boardroom tables around Europe and the Middle East. To say there was a learning curve would be a wild understatement. It wasn't so much of a curve as a mountain-climb.

But if you genuinely believe that you're building a better future for yourself and your loved ones, the pressures are worth it. I've always believed that every decision you make should take you a bit closer to whatever goals, big or small, that you've set yourself. Every night in bed before I go to sleep, I try to review what I've done that day and ask myself whether or not I got even one step closer to where I'm heading. I guess you'd say I'm 'driven' and that's fine. I suppose I'm just curious to see where the boy from the council estate can go. Anything wrong with that?

I got out of the cab. The building loomed before me, a great slab of concrete soaring above the East River.

'There you go buddy,' said the cab driver. 'Enjoy your tour.'

I was gagging to tell him that I wasn't a tourist, but that would have been a bit up myself. I could hardly believe it anyway. Jordan Wylie was about to address the United Nations in New York.

Well not exactly. Not quite all the nations. I'd been invited to give a talk to delegates from various African and other developing countries on the maritime security challenges they were facing now and in the near future. And it would be in a side conference room rather than that huge, awesome assembly hall, so I'd not be standing where the great leaders of the world had stood. Well you can't have everything. But hey, it was still pretty impressive right? I wondered what Buck, Rocky, Macca and my other old mates from the ships would think of me now. No doubt they'd take the piss big-time.

It was, to put it mildly, one of the high points of the past few years; a time when life has been pretty good in most respects. I work with great people and I've strived to gain their respect. I've got a lot out of the maritime industry and like to think I've given something back.

I finally got my BA Hons in 2014. Mum and Dad were thrilled. Jordan Wylie with a degree. Bloody hell, who'd have thought it? Certainly not one of the teachers who'd taught me back in Blackpool. Mrs Fennell had told me I'd better make it as a footballer because I wouldn't be much good for anything else. To be fair though, she'd said it in a rage after I'd caused a small fire in the science lab while arsing around with a Bunsen burner, spirits and some loo paper.

It didn't take a fortune teller to guess that the major challenge of our time would be the danger of cyber-attack. So after getting my BA, I started on a master's degree in Maritime Security with special emphasis on cyber issues. In Britain alone, this past year has seen assaults which have paralysed the NHS and undermined the confidentiality of Parliament. In the wider world, criminals of all hues, motivated by anything from political ideology to simple greed, have become sophisticated to a terrifying degree. The spectrum of malignant intent is always widening; from tricking your old mum into revealing her bank account details in order to nick a few hundred quid to discovering an enemy's next move to help you win a war. Not to mention possible interference in the democratic elections of another country. The world is still in its infancy in learning how to fight back against this new phenomenon and I reckon that fight will be long and hard.

Obviously my own specialism is still the maritime arena and, in 2015, I set up a campaign called *Be Cyber Aware At Sea*. Founded on the work I was doing for my master's degree thesis, this now provides a wide range of free resources to help educate and protect both international navies and merchant shipping in the face of this embryonic threat. At first it wasn't easy to get people to listen: a Somali pirate was a tangible enemy; a cyber brigand was something else entirely. So it took a while to make them realise that, as I often put it, 'online is the new frontline' and just as dangerous as anything else they've had to battle before. But that attitude changed pretty fast and I'm proud to say that the campaign has already won the support of Her Majesty's Royal Navy and other major stakeholders like GCHQ, P&O Ferries, Inmarsat, Teekay and many more. With easy-to-understand articles, videos, posters and best practice guidelines, our aim is to educate everyone, both seafarers and shore-side staff, in the basics of an area which often seems far too technical and intimidating for the average person. I hope we're on the way to becoming a vital resource for everyone who lives and works on the oceans of the world. In early 2017, we won the best cyber awareness campaign award at the International Cyber Security Conference. A fantastic accolade for all our hard work. And in September of this year, I was also highly commended as an 'unsung hero' for my work on raising cyber security awareness throughout the global shipping industry.

So my life after the ships has become even more hectic than it was before. Obviously, I'd now achieved an income and a standard of living I never imagined possible when I'd left school with two GCSEs and sod-all idea of what to do with myself. I'm now even the owner of a racehorse, which is stabled and trained by the great Jamie Snowden himself. The horse has a posh equestrian name, but we usually call him Barney. Jamie and I often laugh about that wet night on Salisbury Plain. I doubt he ever thought that young

Trooper Wylie would one day be one of his customers.

The world of horse-racing is pretty elitist, which makes it a serious opportunity for networking; these days I might find myself at a dinner table with the CEO of an airline, the owner of a Premier League football club and a member of the royal family. Very different from the lads' nights out I'd been used to in the past. It's probably not a great idea to pour beer over the heads of any of this lot. Certainly not advisable to suggest the 'naked bar' game I'd taken part in so often in the army, where everyone had to strip off and the last one naked has to buy the next round of drinks.

Nor would Jamie Snowden ever have imagined one day walking into Windsor Castle with Trooper Wylie, both of us as guests at the reception Her Majesty The Queen gives every year for the owners of horses running in the Grand Military Gold Cup at Sandown Park. I broke out in a sweat when I found myself plucked from the throng for a brief word with the great lady herself; a chat that rolled on for a good 15 minutes. She's tiny, delightful and what she doesn't know about horse-flesh just ain't worth knowing. It was like having a natter with an auntie, albeit with better jewellery than the average auntie possesses; though you never quite forget she is The Queen. That night, I think I was floating about six inches above the Aubusson carpets.

In 2017, we had a syndicate of four, sponsoring my horse Barney in the Military Gold Cup. All of us were ex-King's Royal Hussars, but then one person had to drop out. We had the bright idea of asking Anne, HRH The Princess Royal if, as Colonel-in-Chief of the regiment, she might step in as the fourth member and we were thrilled when she agreed. Sadly, not only did Barney not win, he actually fell, poor bugger. Luckily HRH took it in her stride, sighing that she never had much luck at Sandown. But good old Barney. For somebody who does nothing much beyond eating hay, farting and going for an occasional gallop, he's been a really great mate, a true four-legged legend.

That chat at Windsor with Her Majesty was about more than just horse-racing. She has enormous respect for her armed forces and clearly enjoys talking to anyone from that background. Even though my military career didn't work out as I'd hoped, I've always said how much it means to me to have been a soldier. That's why I often volunteer as a guide at the Winchester museum of my old regiment, where I'm now on the board of trustees. It keeps the connection alive, a connection I will always value. I get a real buzz out of showing people round, seeing some young kid dazzled by the uniforms, the swords and the sabres or chatting to a guy in his 80s whose visit brings back the memories of his own military service and who, just like me, still values them. And I do it because Mum and Dad always taught me that you should try to be a giver and not just a taker.

I've really had a hell of a lot to be happy about. And I *have* been happy in many ways. To the outside world I was, I hoped, as confident and in command as anyone could be. It always helped that I'm outgoing by nature; I loved meeting new people, not just for the pleasure of their company but for the things they might teach me. So I doubt if anybody else could have guessed there was a dark cloud on my sunny horizon, a cloud that was growing a bit bigger all the time.

In the wake of my Nana's death, I'd promised myself to spend much more time with the folk I loved the most. Sadly, that vow pretty much went down the tubes. My new responsibilities meant that I was hardly at home any more often than when I'd been on the ships in Pirate Alley. I was always on planes, always in hotel rooms on my own instead of being with Laura and Evie. It's surprising how lonely you can feel lolling in a Jacuzzi in some five-star gaff in Dubai.

What is not surprising is that Laura got increasingly fed up with having a partner who was hardly there. These strains had always rumbled under us over the years. And it was useless to deny that I'd become a different guy in so many ways. I guess that I was now addicted to a new way of life and that, try as I might, I couldn't kick the habit of it. But I couldn't expect Laura to sacrifice her own needs to mine. Sadly, at the time of writing this book, we've decided to head in different directions. But the most important thing on which we both agree is that we will always do our best by our beautiful daughter Evie. More than any award, accolade or big business deal, this little girl will always be my pride and joy and my greatest achievement.

How very hard and painful such things are. Yet I know that I just have to go on pushing myself, to see where my journey is going to take me. In this life, you can't ever go backwards. You can choose to stay still, to tread water, but that's not for me. So the only way is forward, whatever it might bring.

Where does this all come from? Maybe it's from Mum and Dad, who always believed that I could achieve anything I really wanted and who sacrificed so much for me. Maybe it was seeing all those guys around me in Blackpool going off the rails and heading nowhere except Strangeways. I'm certainly marked forever by seeing friends die long before their time: Alan Brackenbury and Richard Shearer in Iraq, Jon Neve in a hospital bed. And hey, it might even be lessons learnt from those amazing years fighting back against Somali piracy. I remember that rocket-propelled grenade that whizzed past the bridge and nearly blew us all to bits. I remember the tragic stories of the hostages held to ransom, especially the ones who never saw the light again. I even think of the sad tale of the pirate who drowned on his way home from a hijack and was washed up on the beach, still clutching his share of the loot in the plastic bag.

However strong you think you are, you can never know what's coming at you out of a clear blue sky. Our life is a transient thing. So while I've got it, I'm going to ride it for all I'm worth. Like Barney, that racehorse of mine, I'm going hell for leather down that track. Whatever hurdles are thrown up, I'll not shy away from them and, if I land flat on my arse, that's fine. I've done that more than once. Failure is often the spur to success, so I'll just re-mount and have another go until I leap over them. It's only what's in front that matters. What else is there?

This year, on Remembrance Day, Dad and I will walk through the streets of Blackpool, wearing our medals, as we've done for several years now. Just a couple of old soldiers. And I'll keep on looking for ways to make him proud of me.

CHAPTER 19

Resurgence

When the number of hijacks fell off a cliff in 2012, the majority of the 10,000 or so Brits who'd made a mint as private security contractors started flying home like some huge flock of migrating birds. But this didn't mean that the Gulf of Aden and the Indian Ocean had suddenly stopped being dangerous places. As long as the wider Middle East remained arguably the most volatile corner of the world, the seas around it were never going to be as safe as the village duck pond. Vigilance was still needed on any ship that crossed Pirate Alley.

Despite the fact that, in my biased opinion, private security had been the major component in tipping the scales against the pirates, the unease felt by many about armed guards on merchant shipping continued. That whiff of 'mercenary' had never entirely blown away. The issue was, of course, the carrying of weapons. It took the USA and UK governments till 2012 to authorise their use on any vessel sailing under their flags. It was difficult not to raise your eyes to heaven. Only when the worst had passed, did they acknowledge the undeniable success of that strategy.

But the nagging worries about trigger-happy ex-soldiers lingered on. How many weapons, authorised or not, were rattling around in the storerooms of PMSCs in the ports of the Middle East? How much ammo? Now that most of the disciplined British guards had thrown in the towel, what sort of people would have access to these arsenals? All of this was complicated further by a spaghetti-mess of local rules and regulations, which differed from country to country, but some of which banned the presence of guns and ammo within their waters.

As chance would have it, it was the founder of Sovereign Global who came up with some sort of answer with the creation of the 'floating armoury.' This would be a ship, usually about the size of a small frigate, which would act both as a seaborne 'hotel' for those security teams still working in the field and as a secure firearms store to provide the equipment they needed for their next transit through Pirate Alley. The big advantage was that a floating armoury would be located in international waters, all the weapons would be out at sea and no complex national jurisdictions could apply to it. When a ship in need of protection passed close to the floating armoury, the security team it had arranged to hire would simply transfer across to it, armed and ready. When they'd escorted it safely through the high risk area, the team and its weapons would simply disembark onto another floating armoury. They'd then hop aboard the next ship which wanted protection going in the other direction. It was a good theory and it caught the imagination of many maritime security companies. Eventually it's estimated that there were probably around 20 of these vessels dotted around the Indian Ocean each carrying up to 1,000 weapons.

Not surprisingly, there was some international hand-wringing about this new concept. But as the creators of the idea, we put our best efforts into making it as well-regulated and strictly controlled a service as possible. The government of Djibouti became the only state to license these new installations and, on Sovereign's own two armouries, we were supported by Djibouti government officials from the national security agency, coastguard and navy to oversee the storage and movement of all 'controlled goods'.

However Sovereign could only be expected to keep our own house in order. And just as in the first days of Somali piracy there had been a lot of sloppy practices in the use of guards on ships, so the bright idea of the floating armoury also began to suffer from the same shoddy ways. Dodgy stuff like the verified ownership of weapons being a bit vague, weapons not being in the location where they were supposed to be, above all the illegal swapping or hiring out of guns between security companies (many of whom were not British and subject to British law). The old concern soon resurfaced: how many weapons were now floating around the countries bordering the Indian Ocean, either on land or sea? Nobody knew. It was that old 'Wild West' thing again. Not wanting to be associated with any of it, Sovereign Global, having spent seven years lobbying for an internationally recognised standard for floating armouries, sadly but firmly turned its back on its own concept in 2017. From now on, we'd concentrate on helping governments in developing countries to increase their abilities and capacities in security issues, both on land and at sea.

One sad legacy of the lack of regulation around floating armouries still haunts everyone who ever worked in maritime security around the Indian Ocean. In 2013, a floating armoury ship, the *Seaman Guard Ohio*, was intercepted by the Indian coastguard just inside Indian territorial waters, into which it seems to have innocently encroached due to bad weather conditions. It was run by an American company and carried 35 men, many guns and a very large store of ammunition. Though the ship could show legal documentation to prove its weapons were fully licensed, that wasn't enough. In 2016, everyone on the *Seaman Guard Ohio* was sentenced to five years in an Indian jail. The crew included six Britons, now known as the Chennai 6, who are still languishing in truly grim conditions, while the opposing governments go on arguing about the rights and wrongs of the case. I've long been involved in the campaign to keep the Chennai 6 in the public eye, making a video about the case and running a 10k race this year in India to raise funds for their families to visit them in prison. Recently, I was thrilled to get a letter from one of the lads, telling me that the campaign to free them was the hope to which they all clung.

The case of the Chennai 6 is a tragic reminder of risks run by everyone who has been involved in the struggle against the pirates of Somalia, from the first years of the new Millennium right up to the present day. 'Goodies' and 'baddies' alike. The pirate washed up on the beach with his bag of money. The crewman on the *Iceberg-1* who took his own life rather than face one more day of captivity. There but for the grace of God…

They're smug bastards as a rule. Those irritating people who love to say 'I told you so'. And I really hate to enlist in that particular regiment but, well, I told you so. It seems like Somali piracy may be on the rise once more.

On March 13th 2017, a South African oil tanker called the *Aris 13* was seized off the coast of northern Somalia. It was the first successful hijack in five years. Rumour had it that Big Mouth, the notorious pirate leader from the bad old days, was behind it from his prison cell in Belgium. It's believed the ship had no security guards, was travelling at only five knots and wasn't registered with any of the emergency security agencies who could have sent immediate help. Despite all this, the crew was lucky. The pirates discovered that the ship was carrying goods for powerful Somali business interests who they didn't want to offend. Then, when the attack was finally detected, the Puntland maritime police blazed in and surrounded the ship. After a frightening gun battle and tense negotiations, they released the vessel and her crew a few days later without any ransom being paid. Good news, but the damage had been done.

Naturally, everyone hoped it might be a freak incident, but just a week or so later, a large dhow named the *Casayr II* was seized with the worrying suspicion it would be used as a mothership for further attacks. Soon after, two Indian and Pakistani vessels were hijacked within 48 hours of each other and taken to those familiar old pirate havens on the Somali coast. By now, the alarm bells were echoing through the plush offices of the shipping companies and their insurers. The menace that had been slumbering in the depths for so long, had woken and burst back up through the surface.

Since the last major attack in 2012, many in the shipping industry have made an understandable, but fatal, mistake. Like the owners of the *Aris 13*, they've become complacent, taken their eye off the ball. On many vessels, those basic protective measures have been scaled down; the razor-wire allowed to get rusty and the hoses not maintained. Crew training sessions haven't been held as often as before. Or they've begun to sail much closer to the coast and, to save fuel, are travelling more slowly again. Their security guards, if they have any at all, are far less well-paid and less well-trained than the crack-shot ex-forces Brits of the Gold Rush times. Instead of the £500 a day which Rocky, Macca and I used to trouser, some of these guys will be lucky to get £200 a month. At the height of Somali piracy, I reckon about 60 per cent of merchant ships had started to carry armed guards. By 2017, I'd guess it had shrunk to 25 per cent at best. In short, the shipping industry has been sleeping soundly in its cosy bunk, believing that maritime piracy off Somalia is history. Wrong decision.

Worse yet, even the international naval forces have by now eased off their efforts; after all, there are plenty of other problems that need their attention, not least the soaring refugee crisis in the Mediterranean. In late 2016, NATO ended its anti-piracy *Operation Shield*. There were still pockets of piracy off the Gold Coast of West Africa and in the South China Seas but, in the case of Somalia, it seemed that the job was pretty much done. So, in 2017, much of the world's merchant shipping fleet is once again sailing into Pirate Alley in as vulnerable a position as it had done a decade before.

So where have the pirates been since 2012? What have these bad boys been up to? The joint success of the naval forces and of private security teams had certainly decreased their job opportunities. Some just went back to being the simple fishermen they'd been before. Others probably became involved in the people-smuggling trade. For most Somali pirates, the need to earn a living, however despicable the means, is still desperate. For the last few years, they've probably just scraped by. If they'd ever made much money in their pirate heyday, they've probably blown it long ago on fast cars, fast women and their daily expenditure on khat.

But that doesn't mean they no longer have the capability to strike again. The manpower is still there; though large numbers of the original pirates have died, usually by drowning, there are plenty of young guys more than ready to step into dead men's shoes. Behind the scenes, the criminal networks are still there too, more than willing to rev the whole thing up again if the circumstances look favourable. Nor will that be difficult. The *modus operandi* is hardly complex; the few skiffs, the grappling hooks and the rope ladders, the guns and the grenades. And hey, back in business.

The reasons behind the resurgence of 2017 haven't changed either. It's groundhog day. The conditions that drove the spectacular outbreak of Somali piracy between 2008 and 2011 are still present. Today, Somalia still holds the unenviable title of the most fragile state in the world. It's now a whole quarter-century since the outbreak of the Somali civil war. For all these years, its people have been trapped aboard a roller-coaster of political upheaval, economic chaos, tribal conflict and terrorism. Children have grown to adulthood never having known anything else. At sea, the old issue of foreign fishing fleets poaching and damaging fishing stocks in Somali waters has emerged again, as passionately as ever.

If any country deserves some good luck, it's Somalia. Hopes are high for the new government of President Farmajo, a charismatic leader whose election in February 2017 has inspired many Somalis to feel that some sort of turning point has been achieved at last. In Mogadishu, the depressing vistas of war-damaged buildings are now cheered here and there by some hipster cafes and restaurants. After so many grim years, there is cautious cause for optimism. The economy has seen some green shoots of growth and increasing numbers of Somalis who fled the country in search of a better life are returning to rebuild it, bringing their skills with them. And President Farmajo promises a renewed fightback against the terrorism and corruption that have continually undermined the country's previous efforts to pull itself out of the mire.

But the road ahead will be tough. One of Donald Trump's first acts was to include Somalia on his notorious list of Muslim countries from which immigrants would be banned from entering the USA. This is still a violent nation of roadside bombs, suicide bombers and political assassinations. Al-Shabaab has not vanished; it still carries out frequent attacks in Mogadishu and in other parts of the country. Unemployment and poverty are the perfect carrots to tempt aimless young men into extremism – and perhaps piracy. Nearly three-quarters of the population are under the age of 30 and they want to have a future. If their country can't provide one for them, they will go out and find one for themselves, wherever that might lead them.

There can be few leaders in the world with a tougher job to do than President Farmajo. So it's doubly sad that the fates have now thrown more misfortune on this fragile country. The worst drought for decades has hit eastern Africa, decimating crops, killing three-quarters of the country's livestock and bringing the threat of widespread famine and outbreaks of diseases like cholera. Somalia is spiralling downwards into a major humanitarian crisis. Hundreds of thousands of starving people from the parched countryside are flooding into the cities, desperate for help. It's said that a million kids are at risk of malnutrition.

Thankfully, the outside world is doing its best to help. It has already given $600 million to combat the famine and, in May 2017, at the Somalia Conference in London, the international community pledged itself to support the new government; not just by reacting to the emergency of the drought, but by an ongoing programme of assistance to stabilise democracy, improve human rights, tackle terror- ism and the many other blights that Somalia has suffered for as long as most folk can remember. One of those blights is piracy.

I said above that the mostly Sri Lankan crew of the *Aris 13* had been 'lucky'. But that's not quite true of course. They've lived to tell the tale but, like most victims of piracy, they'll never be quite the same people again. As the gun battle began that eventually led to their freedom, it was reported that they'd been forced to call their families in Sri Lanka to say a final goodbye. At the other end of the line, distraught wives and mothers could hear the firing, not knowing if their loved one would still be alive one minute later. The torture of such a thing can surely only be fully understood by those who've gone through such hell.

Of course it's just the same scene which had happened

aboard the *Iceberg-1* years earlier, when the captive crew, imprisoned for almost 1,000 days, had been allowed to call their nearest and dearest for one last time. On that occasion, the nightmarish prospect had been of having their organs ripped from their bodies. On the *Aris 13*, it would have been a swift bullet in the head. The psychological impact of these horrors on the world's seafarers should never be minimised or in any way forgotten. The rest of us depend on these people for so many of the things we take for granted, so we surely owe them that at least.

In the renewed spate of pirate attacks in the spring of 2017, one interesting thing has emerged. Not every single ship in the merchant navy has become complacent and gone back to its sloppy old ways. Not every captain and crew are willing to risk their lives in the interests of saving time or cutting costs. The Lebanese bulk carrier *OS 35* is one such vessel and when it was attacked in the Gulf of Aden, every member of the Filipino crew still knew exactly what to do. They made it to their Citadel, sent out their distress calls and stayed there safely till warships of both the Indian and Chinese navies arrived the next day. By then, the pirates had abandoned their attempt and just melted away across the sea. It is a textbook case which proves that the practices we'd had imposed five years earlier are still as effective as ever.

So it seems that the recent remission in Somali piracy is over and that the disease has struck again. But at least this time, we know how to combat it. As this book goes to press, nobody knows what might now happen. But one thing's for sure. The merchant ships of the world need to be on red alert. Order the razor-wire. Prime the high-

Also by Mirror Books

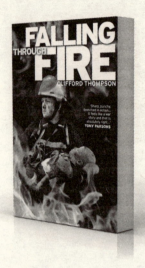

Falling Through Fire
Clifford Thompson

The true story of a London firefighter, now journalist, and his involvement in domestic and high-profile disasters across 25 years.

One incident, early in his career, had a profound effect on him that he carries to this day.

In a frank and honest way he recounts his personal experience of the 1988 Clapham train crash, the 1993 bombing of New York's World Trade Centre and the aftermath of the King's Cross fire.

Clifford describes the trauma that firefighters deal with on a daily basis – and reveals that despite facing many horrific situations and experiencing major disasters, he cannot escape the haunting memory of a three-year-old boy dying in his arms after a house fire just days before Christmas.

Also by Mirror Books

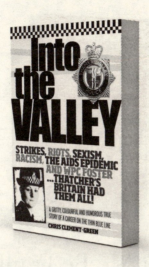

Into the Valley
Chris Clement-Green

Encouraged by the sizeable pay increase and high divorce rate,
Chris Clement-Green decided that answering a recruitment ad for the
Thames Valley Police was just the thing for a much-needed
overhaul of her life.

It was 1984, a time before political correctness, at the height of the miner's
strike and in the middle of five years of race riots. Expanding her police
knowledge and her social life, while undeterred by sexist remarks and
chauvinists, she decided to make her mark.

Chris captures the colourful characters and humour in many of the
situations she found herself in, but the job had its serious side, too. She was
at the centre of a riot in Oxford, during which her life was threatened, and
she worked with victims of rape and sexual abuse.

An often humorous, always candid and no-holds-barred memoir of a
policewoman in the 80s, this book is a personal account of a life in uniform.

Mirror Books

Also by Mirror Books

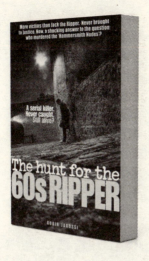

The Hunt for the 60s Ripper
Robin Jarossi

While 60s London was being hailed as the world's most fashionably vibrant capital, a darker, more terrifying reality was unfolding on the streets. During the early hours a serial killer was stalking prostitutes then dumping their naked bodies. When London was famed for its music, groundbreaking movies and Carnaby Street vibe, the reality included a huge street prostitution scene, a violent world that filled the magistrate's courts.

Seven, possibly eight, women fell victim – making this killer more prolific than Jack the Ripper, 77 years previously. His grim spree sparked the biggest police manhunt in history. But why did such a massive hunt fail? And why has such a traumatic case been largely forgotten today?

With shocking conclusions, one detective makes an astonishing new claim. Including secret police papers, crime reconstructions, links to figures from the vicious world of the Kray twins and the Profumo Affair, this case exposes the depraved underbelly of British society in the Swinging Sixties. An evocative and thought-provoking reinvestigation into perhaps the most shocking unsolved mass murder in modern British history.

Mirror Books